Breathe Easy

Paul Arnold

Strategic Book Publishing and Rights Co.

Strategic Book Publishing and Rights Co.
12620 FM 1960, Suite A4-507
Houston, TX 77065
www.sbpra.com

ISBN: 978-1-60976-336-7

DEDICATION

I would like to dedicate this book to my wonderful wife, Melissa.

ACKNOWLEDGEMENTS

I would like to thank those people who have given the subject of organ donation some thought and have decided whether they would like to donate their organs at the end of their life. Obviously a very special thanks to those who then decided they would like to—they truly are heroes and heroines and literally are lifesavers.

I would also like to thank those people who give blood. Both Melissa and Miles have received blood transfusions, as do hundreds of other patients every day. Yet again, those people are lifesavers.

Another thank you goes out to all those mothers who have kindly donated breast milk in the neonatal wards.

My final thank you is a more personal one, and it comes with a big hug and best wishes too. Angela Davis, Melissa's lung consultant, was just about the best person we could have had dealing with Melissa. She had experience in LAM patients from her time spent in America and not many people in the UK have any experience with LAM patients. She made us feel like we were in such good hands throughout Melissa's treatment.

The names of the hospital staff used in this book are fictional to preserve anonymity, including Angela Davis.

BACKGROUND

This blog was written by me. I am Paul Arnold, born in 1973, and I married Melissa on 1 July 2006. It was, without question, the happiest day of our lives.

We had met about eight years previous to the wedding day. Throughout our time together, our love grew stronger and stronger.

Our careers also grew.

I was working at a quantity surveying practise. I had previously taken time out of this occupation to work for six months in the ski resort of Val D'Isere as a pianist and barman. I returned for a few months before resigning to travel around Australia and parts of Asia. I started to realise that I could make money as a pianist and when I returned home, I sought piano work. I left the quantity surveying firm on good terms, and when they had very busy periods, they called me in on an hourly rate. It helped us both out. It was at this point I met Melissa, and since then my career as a musician has continued to make progress (albeit slow progress!).

Melissa, born in 1975, had taken on jobs that were a means to an end until she found a job helping at a dog-grooming parlour. The wages were poor but she learned a lot and simultaneously gained qualifications through a part-time course.

We had been living together for quite a long while before we bought a property together in Buntingford, Hertfordshire. We had started practically living together at my mum and dad's house, although I suppose "officially," Melissa was still living at her mum and dad's house.

My mum fell victim to cancer in 1998. She had given me everything anyone could ask for as a mother, and I am so very grateful for that. Soon after, along with a friend of mine, I bought a property in Hertford. It was a bit early in our relationship to commit to buying a house together—we had only been together for a year or so. Melissa lived there with us, but it was far from ideal.

She convinced me to agree to her getting a dog. I'm so glad she did this. We picked up Karma from a dog home nearby. She was a mongrel with strong signs of Staffordshire bull terrier and Labrador, and she was lovely.

Melissa needed to get away from the bachelor pad and went into a housing association flat. I was often round there with her, and it was nice to have the privacy. She was not there for too long before we bought the Buntingford property together.

It was at our new home that Melissa set up her own dog grooming business and very gradually, she managed to develop a good client base, mainly due to word of mouth.

Melissa also enjoyed all the things she could wish for in her mum and dad, Chris and Frank. Her older brother, Spen, and her younger sister, Lucy, also enjoyed this fantastic upbringing. Chris worked as a cook for the post men and women when I first knew her, and Frank was a carpenter by trade, although he did a lot of general building work in his business (and at home what with extensions and conservatories). Spen had worked for a sign writing company before training himself up with "The Knowledge" in order to successfully become a London cab driver. He met the lovely Tanya. Lucy followed in her sister's footsteps by finally deciding that working with animals was for her. She took a crash course in dog grooming with ideas of one day working with her big sister. At the time of writing this blog, she was working at our house, having taken over Melissa's clients while

Melissa took maternity leave! She had met the lovely Louis (pronounced Lewis, I'll have you know).

Melissa's mum and dad (whom, for the record, I also refer to as Mum and Dad) have always had pets, and at the time I met them, they had two dogs, Daisy, golden retriever, and Poppy, a mongrel, as well as a cat called Carly. They all had good innings but have passed away and now they have Milo, a lovely, rather fat Labrador, and Lenny, the biggest, hairiest cat you could imagine.

My dad married Nikki a while after my mum died. Nikki like my dad, already had two children. They are a great couple. As a nurse, she had the opportunity to live in Australia, and they both took that opportunity and have never looked back. I'm sure they both yearned for a fresh start in their own ways. Nikki's eldest daughter, Josie, stayed in England with her boyfriend. Her youngest daughter, Hayley, went to Australia with them.

Melissa had hearing problems and wore hearing aids in both ears, which did a pretty good job. She also developed epilepsy at a young age. When I met her, she had just changed her consultant to one in London. After a very long process, which included invasive surgery just to test whether she was appropriate or not, she finally undertook brain surgery to remove problematic matter from the brain to eliminate, or at least reduce, the seizures. This amazing surgery took place in January 2005 and it certainly appeared as if it had worked.

So there you have a vague background and history of our lives up to the point of starting this blog.

This blog was originally set up because Melissa and I wanted to inform our relatives and friends of our progress through what was bound to be a difficult pregnancy. At the time of setting the blog up, Melissa had just been diagnosed with Tuberous Sclerosis

Complex and Lymphangioleiomyomatosis (LAM). She was thirteen weeks pregnant.

It was written with my opinions at the time of writing, and, in hindsight, some of these thoughts are not what I think now. I have made mention to these changed opinions in the final chapter.

There are some medical terms that you may not have heard of, and so I have put a glossary of words in Appendix D at the back of the book.

The other Appendices are worth taking a look at before you read the blog to help you understand it.

This book was written to raise awareness of the impact of organ donation. Every year more than 1,000 people in the UK die waiting for a transplant.

If you are not already an organ donor, you can register at www.uktransplant.org.uk.

The profits from the sale of this book will go directly to LAM Action, the registered charity dedicated to research for LAM. Their website is www.lamaction.org.

Melissa

THURSDAY, 30 AUGUST 2007—
GENERAL PICTURE

Okay, hello everyone! We think that it's a good idea to set up a blog for those who want an easy update on our little lives, so here it is.

We are delighted to let you all know that Melissa is pregnant and is now at twenty weeks. We have had lots of scans; the baby looks great and seems to enjoy the upside down headstand position with legs crossed and arms behind head. It looks like it is chilling out or desperate for a wee. The due date is 11 January 2008.

Following the thirteen-week scan, we saw our obstetrician, Gillian. She looked a little perturbed as she ran through Melissa's health history. It was at this moment that she asked for confirmation that Melissa has Tuberous Sclerosis Complex (TSC). We were confused as this was the first we had heard of this, which obviously shocked Gillian. Gillian seemed very concerned and even though we did not have a clue what TSC was, this worried us. At this stage, we all hoped there was just a typing error on the GP's letter where Gillian got this information.

To cut a very long story into just a long one, the GP's letter was correct. Melissa's neuro consultant, Dr Roberts, had kept this piece of information from us for two years, and he still hadn't told us himself. TSC causes lesions to continually grow on the brain, causing seizures; this explains Melissa's history of epilepsy. This also means that she may not be cured indefinitely of epilepsy, as we had thought following her brain surgery in January 2005, since the lesions that were then removed are likely to grow back.

Dr Roberts knew that Melissa has TSC and that we were family planning.

TSC is genetic, and there is a one in two chance of the baby having it.

We have discovered that Melissa has had a mild form of TSC. Should the baby inherit the gene that causes TSC, there is no way of telling whether he or she would have a mild strain or a severe strain. Severe symptoms would include learning difficulties and other more serious mental disabilities.

There are a few procedures that can indicate for sure that the baby has TSC but none that can tell us for sure that the baby does not have it. So far, nothing is showing signs of the baby having TSC. For example, we were sent to Great Ormond Street Hospital for a scan of the baby's heart. The specialists there told us the heart looked normal. Often with TSC there are abnormalities shown on heart muscle. This was great news, but this does not mean the baby definitely does not have TSC.

Melissa has developed Lymphangioleiomyomatosis (LAM), a rare interstitial lung disease. This has only now been diagnosed due to a connection with breathing difficulties and TSC. Apparently 40 percent of females who have TSC also have LAM. Melissa has been complaining of breathing problems that were, until recently, put down first to asthma and then to an unknown interstitial lung disease. Once the specialist knew of the diagnosis of TSC, they immediately diagnosed LAM. LAM primarily occurs in women of childbearing age.

This is already causing major breathing difficulties at this relatively early stage of pregnancy. It is likely that the baby will be delivered early (caesarean) to prevent Melissa going through labour. This procedure would normally take place two weeks before the natural due date.

We've certainly had some surprises to deal with recently. Not only are we worried about Melissa's health but the baby's health too. Moreover, just to top it all off, we were told that LAM patients are advised against pregnancy. We can already see why.

For now, Melissa has been prescribed steroids to help ease her breathing difficulties. She has an oxygen machine installed at home to aid her breathing every now and then. This is in the lounge, and she usually uses it when she watches television in the evenings.

That's a basic picture of where we stand at the moment. I guess the main reason for this blog is to just inform those interested in the progress of Melissa's pregnancy and general health. So I'll leave the story so far there! We'll try to update with new posts after each hospital appointment (pretty regularly then). Next week we have an appointment with the epilepsy nurse at Addenbrookes and a twenty-week scan with Gillian. I will explain why and what happened after the event. I've had enough typing now!

x

WEDNESDAY, 5 SEPTEMBER 2007

We saw our epilepsy specialist nurse, Christina, today at Addenbrookes, and this was quite useful.

Having weaned off the epilepsy medication (as discussed with Dr Roberts before the brain surgery in January 2005), we were told about a month ago by Dr Roberts to go back onto the medication, albeit a small dose, just to keep any possibility of seizures happening again at a lower risk. Confused? We were! Christina thought it was wise to be on a low dose—it was better for us to hear that from her. Any trust we may have had in Dr Roberts has vanished.

Melissa will increase her intake from 150 mg daily to 300 mg of Oxcarbazepine (put into perspective, a couple of years ago the dose was well over 1000 mg AND supplemented with the add-on drug, Keppra). Christina explained that the steroids will be affected by this increase and will have to be closely monitored by her, Melissa's lung specialist, and Melissa.

Christina talked of Melissa's necessity to take Vitamin K from thirty-six weeks. This will be in the form of tablets. The baby will have a Vitamin K injection once born.

The painkiller to avoid during labour is Pethadine (this drug could bring on a seizure) although this is probably not relevant to us because Melissa probably won't be going through labour.

She mentioned that there is a TSC nurse, possibly, in Watford. She will look into it.

That's about it. We have to get some blood tests done in a fortnight at the GP and get results sent to Christina due to the increase in Oxcarbazepine.

Scan tomorrow with Gillian, and I will post the outcome.
Bye for now.

x

THURSDAY, 6 SEPTEMBER 2007

We went to see Gillian today. She is lovely! She makes us feel like we are in such good hands.

We talked about delivering the baby early. At thirty-seven weeks, delivery would still be considered as full term. Thirty-four weeks would be the earliest they would like to deliver. The reason early delivery was discussed is because at thirty weeks the baby will rise up and press against the lungs and reduce their capacity. What with Melissa's current problems, this could prove to be very difficult to deal with. It will be assessed at the time. Premature birth could cause lung problems to the baby, as lungs are the last organs to develop in the womb.

At the twenty-eight-week scan, Gillian is likely to give Melissa prophylactic steroids for her lungs and possibly also give her a Betamethasone steroid injection (the former won't penetrate into the placenta, but the latter will). The Betamethasone is designed for the baby—to help the baby's lungs.

LAM also causes angiomyolipomas (AMLs) on the kidneys. These are a little bit like cysts. The AMLs on Melissa's kidneys measure in at 2 cm, so there is no real risk of them bleeding during pregnancy. At 4 cm, there would be risk of the AMLs bursting, causing internal bleeding.

Prostaglandins, used to soften the cervix, cannot be used on Melissa as it affects the lungs.

The great news (we think?) is that Melissa is fertile. There are seventy people in the UK who have LAM, and half of those are infertile!

So to the scan—billed as twenty week, but Melissa is actually twenty-two weeks. The scan was superb! The baby was doing somersaults, and we saw some great poses. Then we caved in and enquired about the sex. Gillian laughed, suggesting it was pretty obvious—a baby boy!!

Everything looked normal, and we were all smiles.

Next week:

Monday is a biggie—we go to Sheffield to get our little boy MRI scanned to see if there are any tubers at this stage on his brain. This is yet another way of indicating whether he may have inherited TSC. Again, it cannot prove he doesn't have it, only that he has. This is mentally challenging for us. We are of two minds whether these tests are worth it. At the moment, we think we would prefer to know if he has got TSC so that we have time to prepare for it. Although we know what mild TSC involves (as Melissa has that), we are not too clued up on what severe TSC causes. We both also sometimes think why are we bothering—it's not like we will love him any less whatever genes he has, and worrying now will not help any of us.

Thursday we're back to Addenbrookes to see the lung specialist.

x

MONDAY, 10 SEPTEMBER 2007

We are over the moon at the moment!

We went to see Dr Grintham yesterday at Sheffield's Royal Hallamshire Hospital to get the baby's head scanned for abnormalities.

Melissa went to have her head X-rayed first to make sure there were no metal objects left in her brain after her surgery. Then she was put into this big MRI machine. It looked a bit like a space capsule from a Woody Allen movie.

Anyway, the MRI showed no abnormalities on the baby's brain! Fantastic. We saw some amazing images of the baby too and Dr Grintham is going to email some of them.

This is great news but, as with anything we can do, not a definitive sign that baby does not have TSC. However, Dr Grintham did say that those showing nothing at this stage and ending up with TCS, had it mild. (There are only a handful of patients to base this fact on).

We felt relief and had big smiles. We both went down the pub and got hammered. Well actually, I did some tiling, and Melis cooked dinner and watched TV, but the pub was where we were mentally.

Lung specialist Thursday.

x

Thursday, 13 September 2007

We went to see Prof. Wendall, lung specialist, today.

It appears that in his experience, steroids have never helped LAM and immediately suggested Melissa wean off the drug. He suggested that it might be helping the asthma, which could be what makes Melissa feel better on a certain dose. Melissa is going to come off the steroids 1 mg at a time in five-day periods. Steroids are not very nice things, and it would be much better if they can be avoided.

The great news is that there are drugs coming out around now that appeared to prevent LAM from progressing. Prof. Wendall thought we were just in time to be helped by them. We need to get the pregnancy out of the way first though.

We all know how Melissa likes taking at least twenty pills in the mornings, so this should make her feel at home (for those that weren't aware, Melissa used to throw handfuls of tablets down her throat to help control epilepsy).

Prof Wendall informed us that LAM is a progressive disease but not rapidly so. He said Melissa has mild to moderate LAM at the moment. The pregnancy hormones are affecting the situation. This is good and bad news. Good news because it means Melissa will probably start to feel better after pregnancy before the gradual progression of the disease (the progression might be stopped with this new medication?!). Bad news because there is a 40 percent risk of Melissa having a Pneumothorax. This is where a cyst-type thing on the lungs, caused by LAM, bursts. The lung collapses, and we would need to get to Accident and Emergency (A+E) to drain the lung and then get specialist advice.

We will be writing up a note to pass to the A+E team if we ever end up there because we won't remember all this tomorrow, let alone in a month's time!

The AMLs on the kidneys could grow quicker because of the pregnancy hormones, so these will be monitored.

The confusion about the oxygen machine that we have in our lounge at the moment was cleared up. At one stage, because it didn't seem to have any real impact on Melissa after use, there was a question mark over whether Melissa's problem could be in connection with not properly expelling carbon dioxide (that is, NOT a lack of oxygen). This would have rendered the oxygen machine a waste of time—and possibly even dangerous! Professor Wendall clarified that the oxygen intake would do no harm and would probably be good for the baby.

Neurologist next week.

x

THURSDAY, 20 SEPTEMBER 2007

We went to Addenbrookes today—who'd have guessed?

We went to see Dr Gifford, neurologist. It was mainly just to touch base as Melissa will now be under his care and everything will be transferred from King's College Hospital.

Nothing much to say really.

It was great to hear him say that, having gone from many seizures to none as a direct result of the surgery, and due to the fact that once Melissa came off of all medication, there was still no sign of seizures, it was pretty unlikely that epilepsy would return.

He said that going back on to 300 mg per day of the anti-epilepsy drugs was a mere precaution due to pregnancy, and this would be reviewed after the birth.

Thankfully, we have a three-week break from visits to Addenbrookes. We are back there on 11 October—four appointments that day! It's a nice touch that each specialist is trying to arrange appointments on the same day, based on the logic that one long visit is easier for us than several separate ones.

This is very true. Melissa finds it pretty difficult getting out and about.

x

THURSDAY, 11 OCTOBER 2007

10:00 DR PELGRUM, RENAL SPECIALIST

Ultrasound scan on kidneys looks as expected for someone who has TSC. The AMLs on the kidneys are all less than 2 cm in diameter. This does not concern Dr Pelgrum. Kidney failure is highly unlikely.

We booked next scan and consultation in for mid 2008. If the cysts have not grown, appointments can be every five years.

12:00 GILLIAN

We reviewed that thirty-four weeks is initial target before caesarean. This depends on how long Melissa's lungs can deal with the pregnancy that will be progressively pushing up on her lungs.

Steroid injections for Melissa's placenta will be administered four weeks prior to caesarean. This is to ensure the baby's lungs are strong enough if he comes out that early. We booked this in for 23 October.

13:40 GILLIAN—ULTRASOUND SCAN

We saw some lovely images of our little boy!

Gillian made some worrying observations on the baby's brain. The 'horns' at the front end of the ventricle passage were prominent. She was not convinced it was TSC related because it was the same on both sides and fairly symmetrical.

Then Gillian also observed that the area at the back of the brain where the two hemispheres connect appeared fine near the top of the brain, but lower down towards the spine, the hemispheres were not so connected. There is concern that something is missing here—part of the brain that affects balance and co-ordination.

She did say that it was unusual to be closely studying these parts of the baby's brain at this stage, so perhaps these judgments were too early to call.

On her report, Gillian mentions Agenesis of the corpus callosum (ACC). We have since looked this up on the web, and it seems that ACC can in fact show up prominent ventricle horns and partial or complete absence of corpus callosum. There are possible connections to genetic disorders but no real mention of TSC in these. All sounds a bit ominous. We walked away with plenty on our minds.

16:00 PULMONARY LUNG FUNCTION TEST

This test showed that Melissa's lung capacity was reasonable, but oxygen transfer was running at 50 percent of what it should be. Melissa's oxygen levels in her blood are low.

16:30 ANGELA DAVIS, LUNG SPECIALIST

General progress check-up on how Melissa is doing with her breathing.

It was discussed that Melissa seems to be better when sitting down but needs oxygen when moving about. Melissa now has portable oxygen tanks. They are light and fit into a neat little backpack. She gets a few looks when she is out and about but also a lot of people go out of their way to help her with bits and pieces.

Angela is our lung specialist who works with Prof. Wendall. She has experience with LAM patients from her time spent in America and has a particular interest in this disease. We are extremely lucky to have her at Addenbrookes.

Back at home, we had a cup of tea, but we're stressed, confused, and tired. Nice weekend planned to take our minds of things for a bit. Meal/band/comedian evening has been booked at Hunters Meet, Hatfield Heath on Friday night. I have a local gig on Saturday, so I'll be home early for some time together.

x

SATURDAY, 13 OCTOBER 2007

12:00. We were at home and I was just finishing some grouting in the bathroom (this seems to have been going on ages, and I haven't started laying the floor tiles yet!). Melissa had her sister Lucy, with a dog that Lucy had just bathed, and her friend Teresa with her downstairs. Suddenly, she felt some pain and needed to sit down. She asked for a hot water bottle. Ten minutes later, she was writhing around on the settee, screaming in agony. I have never really heard Melissa shouting in pain before, so I figured this was pretty serious. It was certainly terrifying for us spectators. An ambulance came fairly promptly, and they decided that although Melissa was under care at Addenbrookes in Cambridge, they would save twenty minutes by driving to A+E at Stevenage, Hertfordshire.

This proved to be a big mistake. Melissa is twenty-seven weeks pregnant and because of this, they drove straight round to delivery ward. A lovely ward with such friendly staff (excuse my dry humour).

First, we saw a midwife who checked on the baby. The baby seemed to be fine. While I tried to explain Melissa's health situation, she told me that she was speaking to Melissa, not me. Right. Melissa could hardly string two words together. Next, the doctor came round. He was difficult to understand, but we managed to get the drift. The baby was okay. Melissa was still in agony, and I asked the doctor about painkillers. He walked out of the room. Did he hear me? Was he going to reappear with some painkillers?

Melissa's family was outside but not allowed in the ward.

I gave the midwife the piece of paper that explained a little bit about Melissa's rare condition. She took it to the doctor. No reaction.

Cue long boring story of turmoil that I won't bother you with. Basically, after three hours, Melissa was given one Paracetamol tablet and left there in agony. I had been ignored throughout. I requested they transfer Melissa to Addenbrookes. Nothing.

Finally, I went outside the ward, found a wheelchair, and walked it through the ward and into Melissa's room. "Wait! Wait! What are you doing?"

My response was, "I'm taking Melissa to somewhere where she'll get care. It's called a hospital. I'm not sure what you call this place."

At about this time, a nurse who really did seem to care had turned up, and things suddenly changed. Painkillers were administered. The transfer request was processed. An ambulance was on the way. The nice nurse was actually talking to us. The family was allowed in to see their daughter/sister. Some blankets were mustered—Melissa was cold and had been for hours. The blankets were not very far away—just along the corridor a bit.

We got to Addenbrookes' Accident and Emergency Ward at some point that evening. Probably between 18:00 and 19:00. A brighter, cleaner hospital with good staff. A lung specialist and a kidney specialist both assessed Melissa. With no definite answers, Melissa was chest x-rayed and then transferred to a chest ward, Ward F6. I left at midnight. Melissa was still in pain and had not much chance of sleep, but at least she was receiving painkillers that were aiding the situation.

x

SUNDAY, 14 OCTOBER 2007

ADDENBROOKES, WARD F6.

Melissa's oxygen levels were very low. They continue to administer painkillers.

Any problem with the kidneys has been ruled out, as has a pulled muscle.

Word from the Maternity Ward (The Rosie) is that Melissa might as well have the steroid injections (so that the baby's lungs will cope with early delivery) and Vitamin K supplement for baby (to counter Melissa's anti-epileptic drugs) while she is in hospital.

Sunday is obviously a day of rest, there's a distinct lack of useful staff!

x

MONDAY, 15 OCTOBER 2007

HAPPY BIRTHDAY, MELISSA! What a fantastic way to celebrate your birthday.

Her breathing was very bad in the morning but got slightly better throughout the day.

The steroid injections are happening, and vitamin K is being taken.

The kidneys, yet again, have been ruled out as a cause of this pain and breathing difficulty.

Melissa then had a CT scan on her heart to check for blood clots.

The results were pleasing. They showed no sign of any blood clot, and they also picked up some clues as to what this problem might be—there appears to be signs of blood in the kidney area.

It also showed that the lower part of the left lung appears to have either a patch of pneumonia or a partial collapse.

An ultrasound scan on the kidneys showed that an AML has burst and caused a large amount of internal bleeding from the kidneys.

Didn't the kidney specialists rule out a problem with the kidneys? Twice? This also makes a mockery of Dr Pelgrum's assessment of the previous kidney ultrasound scan when he said that he was not worried because the AMLs were all less than 2 cm diameter (4 cm is when there is concern). Our next consultation with him is mid 2008! Perhaps the pregnancy has affected this.

The plan is to wait for the bleeding to stop! Genius.

TUESDAY, 16 OCTOBER 2007

ADDENBROOKES, WARD F6.

Melissa is recovering from such an amazing birthday.

The High Dependancy Unit (HDU) team has taken the time to introduce itself.

The blood transfusion team has taken the time to introduce itself.

Melissa's breathing and pain is worse. We can't get over the fact the plan is to do nothing. Melissa is really struggling here. It's hard enough to watch her go through this.

Pneumonia has been ruled out.

x

Thursday, 18 October 2007

Addenbrookes, Ward F6.

Melissa is feeling like shit. She doesn't want to talk to me, or anyone for that matter. She did not get a lot of sleep at all last night. Her head is all over the place. She feels groggy, and she's in a lot of pain.

She had another ultrasound scan on the kidneys. She had to wait an hour for this down in the ultrasound department, and her painkillers were administered late as a result. This did not help the situation. Didn't anyone consider this before she went down? Surely, they could have sent for her when they were absolutely ready to do the ultrasound?

The blood transfusion that took place a little later certainly did help though. A weird thing to go through with. Four hours of someone else's blood feeding into your bloodstream. The new blood has very nice levels of oxygen, thank you very much indeed. We hope it lasts for a bit. Melissa has been in need of some physical improvements for a long while! We appreciate blood donors immensely.

A partial collapse of the lower part of Melissa's lung was ruled out.

x

FRIDAY, 19 OCTOBER 2007

Things are starting to get better!

Arrangements are being made for a transfer to the Rosie (maternity ward), which offers a much more relaxing and caring atmosphere. Melissa is looking forward to a nice sleep more than anything else.

After we were told that the room in the Rosie was being cleaned, we packed up Melissa's things, but by the time I had to leave three hours later, Melissa was still waiting.

x

SATURDAY, 20 OCTOBER 2007

Melissa did not move to the Rosie Ward.

I walked over to the ward and talked to one of the head midwives there. She explained that the staff required to monitor Melissa's observations were not organised in time for the weekend, and they can't risk caring for Melissa because they are not really trained to spot irregularities in the lung observations.

We unpacked. Melissa remains tired.

x

MONDAY, 22 OCTOBER 2007

Oh my goodness, as if the kidney spillage was not enough.

Melissa has had a partial pneumothorax (lung collapse) this morning and has some horrible pains in her right lung.

It was quite a small pneumothorax but with her condition, Melissa felt the effects of it a lot more.

Dr Craddock, championed as the best radiologist in the UK, was not very far away and, even though he was not on call, had agreed to drive over to Addenbrookes to drain the chest cavity of air.

I touched on it before, but I'll try and explain again a little better. Basically, a pneumothrax occurs when air leaks from inside the lung into the area between the lung and chest wall (chest cavity), creating an air pocket. This in turn squashes the lung, forcing the lung into a collapsed state. In order to re-expand the lung, the air needs to be drained from the chest cavity. This is achieved by entering a needle into the cavity, inserting a chest tube, removing the needle (leaving the tube there), and draining the air (sometimes with the use of a suction). It is not usually a massive procedure, one that has previously been carried out on the ward.

In this case, the air cavity was too small for the out-of-hours doctors to want to carry out the procedure (it was after 18:00). In order to get it right, Dr Craddock planned to use a CT scan during the insertion of the needle so that he could be precise enough to hit the right place.

So over came Dr Craddock. The best thing since Frank Zappa. He put the needle in. The air immediately squeezed out before the chest tube was in. The lung immediately inflated and hit the needle. Dr Craddock was not very happy at this point and wanted to make it slightly more on the worthwhile side of things. So he carried on trying to put the tube in anyway. I could hear Melissa screaming from the end of the corridor where I had to wait. I can only assume her lung was still scratching around on the end of a needle. Dr Craddock gave up with the tube and went home. I didn't get the opportunity to thank him for his fine work.

Before he left, he mentioned to Melissa that after a pneumothorax, when the lung re-expands and touches the chest wall again, there would be an unpleasant feeling where the natural mucus-like substance that makes the lung slide against the chest wall is not there anymore. This will take a little while to build back. A couple of hours perhaps.

Perhaps "a couple of hours" for someone whose lungs are in better shape than Melissa's, although in this case, Melissa's pain was likely to have been caused by the elegant needle-scratching episode. So Melissa was in agony for the night. There was no way she could lay on her back. Or side for that matter. So she was exhausted and faced with the prospect of no sleep, just sitting in an upright position on her bed all night, crying. Painkillers were not frequent or strong enough. She probably couldn't even feel the kidney bleed any more.

I had to go home (at about 01:00 in the end). I felt terrible leaving her. I dread to think how Melissa felt.

x

TUESDAY, 23 OCTOBER 2007

Melissa managed to get an hour sleep last night by somehow maneuvering into a very upright position at the head of the bed.

The pain had started to go, but she was now developing a fever. Hot and cold sweats with a dose of diarrhea. What a ridiculous saga this is.

More pain is occurring in the kidneys. This is possibly a kidney infection.

New pain occurred in the left lung—but an x-ray cleared anything nasty there.

The fever was a little better in the afternoon.

The obstetricians have informed Melissa that, if need be, they are ready and comfortable with delivering the baby at any stage now. This pregnancy so far has lasted just over twenty-eight weeks.

Diarrhea persisted throughout the night.

x

WEDNESDAY, 24 OCTOBER 2007

Melissa went for another lung x-ray. All appeared to be okay.
She's been told she could have a urine infection.
The fever continues.

x

Thursday, 25 October 2007

An MRI scan was arranged for this morning. This showed that the kidneys are still bleeding. There is also a likely infection around the kidneys.

Intravenous (IV) antibiotics were administered. Nutrients have been added in the IV antibiotics to get some substance into Melissa's body for the baby (and Melissa!) to feed on. The diarrhea is becoming a serious concern.

Later on Melissa was starting to feel a bit better! Bloody hell!!

Gillian had said that as soon as they think Melissa is in optimum condition, they would intervene with the pregnancy. This basically means that if Melissa continues to feel better each day into early next week, we will be Mummy and Daddy then.

We'd better start thinking of a name!

x

FRIDAY, 26 OCTOBER 2007

Melis was feeling and looking pretty good today (all things considered).

The fever is a bug. One of these hospital super bugs making UK headlines at the moment. We were handed a leaflet about it, but I can't remember what it's called—I'll let you know later. Because Melissa has been on antibiotics, the bug won't go away.

We are really hoping that Melis does not have a setback for a few days. Bringing the baby out must be the best for both him and her.

I like Arlo, but Melis thinks it sounds too much like Harlow (a neighbouring town with a not-so-wonderful reputation). I also can't have Ernie. Fair enough, but Melis can't have Ruben. If he gets my big nose . . .

This could be tricky!

x

SATURDAY, 28 OCTOBER 2007

No setbacks! Come on, keep it up.

The bug is called Clostridium difficile (C-diff). It is preventable by simply keeping the hospital clean!

x

TUESDAY, 30 OCTOBER 2007

Melis has been improving slowly over the weekend. All her pains have gradually been getting easier to cope with.

We were told today that they would go ahead with the caesarean tomorrow. All specialists have been booked in. Just need confirmation that a HDU bed will be available.

Fingers are crossed (although Melis doesn't really like the sound of a Halloween baby!!).

x

WEDNESDAY, 31 OCTOBER 2007

By 08:00, we were all packed up and ready to go. Nervous. Excited. We didn't know what to do with ourselves! Then we were told that there was not a bed available in HDU, but there would be a review of beds there in an hour.

Nine o'clock came and went with no news. We doubted that no news was good news in this case.

At 10:30, Gillian came up to explain to us that it would not happen today. She had put a lot of work into organising today, not to mention the theatre room being completely cleaned out and not in use for a morning. We are getting used to things not quite working out. At least it gives Melis a chance to get rid of the C-diff bug she has had for two weeks now, as it's on its last legs.

And it means we don't have a Halloween baby! I thought that was appropriate myself. Never mind.

x

THURSDAY, 1 NOVEMBER 2007

We were told first thing this morning that there would be a bed available in HDU at noon today. Superb!! Melis is ready. The whole hospital is ready!

So 12:00 turns into 13:00 but we don't care—it was all going to happen this time.

I went down into theatre with Melis. I was given a very fetching garment to wear.

First the anaesthetic—a double epidural. A bit of hit and (a lot of) miss, but the anaesthetist got there eventually. The surgeon, Mr Greenways, was fantastic. Using laser to make the initial cut through the skin produced a clean cut. Then there was a bit of tug-o-war to open the hole into a round shape. A metal clamp was inserted. Just the one cut to the womb was sufficient. I was managing to see most of this amazing work, but Mr Greenways's body was blocking a fair bit. He did however stand back at the right time. Saying, "This one's coming out nicely," he moved out the way, and a lovely little head popped out from Melissa's tummy. Incredible. He put his hands in around the baby's body and brought him out into our world!!

Our baby boy was shown to us both for a quick hello and then whisked away to the side of the theatre room where they had prepared his inspection bed. Melis and I were all smiles. What a feeling. I was called over to cut the umbilical cord (or trim it anyway—it had obviously already been cut from Melis).

I was then a bit of a hazard, floating around, drifting over to have a peak at the placenta. I was quickly told to get back behind the sterile zone. Ooops. I sat back down next to Melis. We were both overjoyed to say the least.

To cap it all off, Melis was already breathing better!

We knew it was coming, but it was still a shame that baby went one way (Neonatal) and Melis went another (HDU).

I got changed and followed Melis to HDU. She seemed great. She was breathing well. Nothing nasty had happened when the pressure had released from her lungs and kidneys. HDU now seems a little over the top. I suppose the logic was better to be safe than sorry.

I nipped over to Neonatal to see baby. He was doing fine. He took the first breath by himself—a good sign for a premie.

He was armed with a C-PAP. This device supplies oxygen through the nose to create a constant air gap to ensure the lungs do not completely close together when he exhales. This makes it easier to breathe. He was also on a drip feed of sugar water.

Back over to Melis. She was looking great. Obviously, she is absolutely gutted that she can't go and see her beautiful creation.

Tomorrow I'll wheel her over, and we'll all be together.

I left and made some phone calls, sent some emails and texts, and generally jumped around the house.

Previously, I had looked forward to the day when Melis was feeling better because I thought then I might get some sleep, but the last thing I want to do now is sleep!!

x

FRIDAY, 2 NOVEMBER 2007

We really are Mummy and Daddy!!!

I popped in to see our baby. He's doing well, nice and cosy in a little incubator with access into the sides via little portholes. He was doing okay with the CPAP device but not as well as he could have been. He's now got a tube down his gob. Can't be that comfortable! Still, I'm assured this is all pretty normal for a premature baby.

He weighed in at 3 pounds ½ ounce.

Then I was straight over to see Melis. She reported a few pains in her kidney area but was still doing well. Remarkable really after the way her organs were behaving before the birth. Unfortunately, before she knew much about it, the lung specialist on HDU injected more epidural. He was not trained to think about Melis wanting to go and see her baby. Melis needed a bed transfer. She just did not fit in at HDU. The lung specialists did not want her on F6 because they were happy that Melissa was over the scary stage of something potentially happening to her lungs, and they did not know anything about epidurals. Midwives, on the other hand, did not want her on the maternity ward because they are not trained to read pulse levels, blood pressure, and other observations they felt Melissa was still in need of. They didn't say so, but we think more to the point was that they had never had C-diff bug over in their ward and didn't want Melis spreading it over there. Basically, no one wanted Melis in the hospital. What a lovely feeling it must have been for her.

I wanted to wheel her over to our baby, but HDU personnel wouldn't allow it. She was under their care and responsibility, and they had to accompany her, which they couldn't because they were way too busy on the HDU ward.

The man opposite Melissa died this morning. That's the fourth death Melis has witnessed since she's been in.

Afternoon came.

The Rosie Ward eventually caved in and said they were preparing a side room for Melissa. At 16:30, we eventually transferred to Delivery Ward, in a room right out of the way and not particularly near Neonatal Ward where our son was residing!!

After an hour, it became quite clear that no one on the ward wanted to go near Melis. We should have painted a big cross on the door.

I had to go to work, very annoyed—I thought all three of us would be together today.

Melissa's mum stayed. Melissa didn't get offered dinner. Not even a cuppa. At 19:00, Gillian came over. Thank goodness because Melis was in tears. She just wanted to see her baby.

Thirty-six hours after the birth of her son, her bed was finally wheeled through to see him. This whole episode was extremely upsetting and frustrating, but all that was forgotten while Melissa saw her son.

x

SATURDAY, 3 NOVEMBER 2007

Melissa was transferred to a bed on Sara Ward, next to the Neonatal Ward, this morning. Of course, she was put in a side room. The lurgy is still feared by all. It is understandable. We are well trained in washing our hands every time we leave the room. The last thing we want is to transfer the bug to others in the ward. So it's guilt and rejection all rolled into one big feeling. Anyway, we stick to the rules, and no one gets hurt!!

Melissa, being Melissa, is already on her feet. Well sort of. She can get to the en-suite toilet without much of a hand.

She got into a wheelchair, and we both went to see our son together. Fantastic. Words just don't work here.

Our baby is looking slightly jaundiced, so he'll be sunbathing tomorrow under lamps. He's doing well though and looks great to me!

x

TUESDAY, 6 NOVEMBER 2007

Okay, I skipped a few days, but you're probably bored by now—I could go on for ages. Melis changed his nappy the other day. I had a go today. It's a bit fiddly—such a small bum. Fitting your hands through the side access holes and trying to avoid all the tubes and ECG leads inside the incubator, to carry out this job isn't that easy. I think I did okay, but I'm sure a little experience will do wonders.

Over the last day or so we have come up with a name: Miles.

It means forgiving! It's an anagram of Melis!! This could get confusing, but it's nice. Miles' grandparents have a dog called Milo. Okay, it's all a bit ridiculous.

We like it though—Miles Joseph Arnold.

Melissa's granddad was called Joseph.

Melis has taken to expressing milk really well. But today we were told that, according to recommendations, the anti-epilepsy medication she is currently on prevents breast-feeding from being on option. Another reason for us to be annoyed at Melissa's old neurologist who put her back on the drug when she was doing fine without it. We doubt he was at all interested in whether the drug would be okay with breast-feeding.

The lung specialists are happy for Melis to return home, as are the kidney specialists. We're just waiting for the obstetrics team to say the same.

I'm really looking forward to snuggling up to someone at night. Anyone will do.

x

That was a joke by the way.

MONDAY, 12 NOVEMBER 2007

Melissa has been at home for a few days now. It's amazing how much more relaxed I feel with a bit of privacy and not rushing about like a lunatic, which is what I was doing when she was in hospital.

Miles is eleven days old today!

He's doing very well. He's been on the CPAP breathing aid for a while now, but twice a day he breathes with no help. He's done a four-hour unaided breathing session recently, although today only managed an hour. He's going in the right direction at his own pace!

He's got a little tube going into his mouth all the way down into his gut. He is being fed donated breast milk. Our thanks go out to all those who donate! The quantity has been going up one-half a millilitre every eight hours, and he's now on 5 ml (taken every hour).

Addenbrookes is now waiting for an available bed in the neonatal unit in Lister Hospital, Stevenage. Miles will then be transferred. This proves that he is doing well. Although we had a very nasty experience at Lister, we feel fairly comfortable with that. We have been assured that the neonatal unit is great there.

I really ought to start thinking about finishing the bathroom tiling at some point!

x

SUNDAY, 18 NOVEMBER 2007

I had a lovely hug with Miles today. He was transferred to Lister Hospital, Stevenage, last Tuesday (13 November). He has not been able to come off the CPAP since the move, but this is thought to be more due to the reflux (bringing up little bits of formula milk) obstructing his airways. They'll be administering some medication to prevent the reflux, and this should enable him to come off the CPAP more regularly.

We are now only twenty minutes away from Miles, and we are starting to feel more relaxed about the whole thing.

I'm afraid to say he appears to have my big nose. Sorry.

x

SUNDAY, 2 DECEMBER 2007

Sorry it's been a while since I updated the blog!

Things are really going well with Miles and with Melis for that matter!

Miles is breathing for nine hours without the CPAP aid and then for three hours with it. This cycle then repeats. That's going up to ten hours without aid tomorrow. I'm sure it won't be too long before he's off it completely. Then they will feed him every three hours (at the moment it's every two hours).

He is 2 ounces short of being a 5 pound baby now! His feeds are up to 33 ml every two hours. He is now being fed NutriPrem2, which is the feed he will come home with.

He moved from the intensive care area into the less stressful HDU area. He has been a high-dependency baby for a while now but only today have they managed to find the space for him in HDU.

His room at home is looking pretty good now. His cot is assembled—just below the dartboard. (Yes, I know, the dartboard *might* have to be removed). Melissa's dad installed some sliding doors, partitioning off a little office area that I'm sitting in now. I was a bit put out with the size at first, but it's actually fine. I've yet to try to set my keyboard up in here, but it looks like it'll fit in with a bit of juggling. Poor me. Miles' room, on the other hand, is massive. I know he's doing well, but I'm not too clear on how he deserved the big room.

Melissa and I ate out last night. We thought we'd get that in before we can't. It was really nice indulging in fine food and plenty of wine (proving Melis is on the mend). Our thanks go to Dad and Nikki for that!

x

THURSDAY, 20 DECEMBER 2007

Melissa had an appointment to see her kidney specialist today. She has been getting some sharp pains recently in the kidney area. While she was at Addenbrookes last week having a lung function test, she thought she would go and try to get an ultrasound scan.

The renal team, as usual, were not helping Melissa (all they had to do was commission an ultrasound). The secretary advised Melissa to wait in A+E and be seen there. After a long day of waiting, the doctor at A+E decided that Melissa should have . . . an ultrasound scan on her kidneys! This eventually happened, but still no one from the renal team came to discuss the results. It was Angela Davis (Melissa's lung specialist) who took it upon herself to find Melissa and at least talk to her about it. She explained that it was unclear whether there was a small new bleed or new AMLs formed where the old hemorrhage occurred. An MRI scan was booked in for Tuesday that Melissa duly attended.

So, today, you would have thought Dr Pelgrum, the kidney specialist, was going to discuss the results of the MRI. Nope. He just told us that the radiographers were still debating what was happening. It's all very new to him, and he would suggest we wait until something happens! Amazing—thanks for your amazing knowledge, doc.

Yet again, it was Angela who came to the rescue. She had been talking to the radiographers and came to us with a definitive diagnosis. Hard to understand why Dr Pelgrum did not have the conclusions at hand.

Angela explained the situation to us. From Melissa's earlier scans on her kidneys, we were told there were little AMLs of no concern because they were less than 2 cm in diameter. These were on the top part of the kidney. It actually turns out that the bit they thought was the top of the kidney was in fact a rather large AML (not the top part of the kidney at all). A kidney is typically 6-8 cm in width and 12 cm long. The AML on Melissa's kidney is 7 cm wide. The blood vessel feeding the AML at times gets near to the surface of the AML and this is what was mistaken for small AMLs. Basically, the renal team got it all wrong from the start. I can understand why Melissa was in so much pain. A cyst-type thing that sat on Melissa's kidney, as wide as the kidney itself, had burst during her pregnancy.

Anyway, what it means is Melissa has a huge AML that not only has already burst once causing Melissa intense pain but also is likely to burst at any time again. Melissa is to either have an operation to remove the AML (and a little bit of kidney to boot) or an operation to embolise the AML (put a coil in the blood vessel that is feeding the AML). Angela is going to discuss with David Goulbourn at Nottingham—he is the leading UK specialist in LAM.

They will also discuss whether David has ever seen AML-looking things that have shown up on the MRI that do not appear to actually be attached to anything but have formed and grown bigger in an area below Melissa's kidneys.

Bring it on.

Miles is completely off the CPAP device now. He is in a cot now (not in an incubator), and he has been promoted to Special Care—the last stop before discharge!! It's great visiting him now. It's so much easier to pick him up, cuddle, feed, cuddle, change nappy, cuddle, wash, and cuddle.

Lovely.

x

SUNDAY, 23 DECEMBER 2007

Miles is home!!! They let the little rascal out yesterday. There was all this talk of needing five days off of everything with no problems before discharge. Then suddenly, after two days, we were called in for an overnight stay in a room at Lister with Miles, so we could get a little familiar with the situation and have any immediate questions answered with a view to all going home together the next day.

I had a gig so joined Melissa and Miles in their own room at about three in the morning. It was great. Miles kept grunting, moaning, and straining, and we spent all night wondering if he was okay. We must have had about two hours sleep—only to be told the next day that all babies do that and there's nothing to worry about! (it would have been quite nice to know that the day before). The following day was all go. The doctor came round for final checks, and finally we were a family together at home.

Absolutely amazing.

Bloody brilliant.

Miles is lovely. We even got a pretty good night's sleep—probably about five hours or so. Just feeding him when necessary and gazing at him when totally unnecessary.

HAPPY CHRISTMAS INDEED!!!

Today has been really nice just chilling out—the three of us. My gig was cancelled for this evening. Bonus! Work is so over-rated.

x

SATURDAY, 5 JANUARY 2008

Happy New Year to everyone!!

We just about stayed awake on New Year's Eve to see it in!

Miles has been amazing. He is now 7 pounds 6 ounces, and he's feeding roughly every four hours—this means we feed him at midnight and only really need to get up once in the night (04:00) to feed him. He has been a gentle introduction to parenthood.

Melissa is not doing so well with her breathing. We went to see Angela Davis. Melissa's breathing throughout the night has been monitored, and the results were okay. During the day, however, things are getting very difficult. The stairs are by far the main problem. At the moment, Melissa has only been using the portable oxygen tank when she is walking around outdoors, but Angela thinks she needs a permanent indoor oxygen machine with a tube long enough to reach to every room in the house. This is being organised.

We then discussed the immediate pursuit of the Rapamycin drug that halts the progress of LAM in most cases and can even reduce the size of the AMLs on her kidneys in a few cases. We were waiting for Melissa's hormones to settle after the pregnancy, and this can usually take six months. Angela was not keen to wait this long. It sounds like a lot of red tape to hurdle in order to obtain this drug, so we'll see how long it is before Melissa has it in her hands. Angela then went on to discuss with us the need to consider having an assessment for a lung transplant sooner rather than later.

It dawned on us more than ever before how much this

pregnancy had appeared to accelerate the disease to a dangerous level.

When Melissa had her invasive brain surgery back in 2005, we both came away thinking that would be the hardest thing she would ever have to go through. How wrong we were. We were now looking at a lung transplant. We were shocked by this news and also apprehensive. We knew nothing about transplants.

Melissa had mild to moderate LAM about nine months ago, and now it was severe, severe enough to talk about a transplant. We knew that the only cure for LAM would be transplantation but never really took that on board at the time we were told.

Melissa bravely asked how long they estimate she'll live as she is. Angela guessed about a year. What can you say to that? We looked at each other. We knew that all our hopes were pinned on a transplant now.

We're going to have a look at the prices of bungalows in the area we live because climbing stairs is already a daunting task for Melissa, although I have a feeling we might be a little shocked!

Miles has his 0th birthday in five days! He seems to have been with us for a long while, yet his due date was 11 January!!

x

THURSDAY, 10 JANUARY 2008

Melissa had an appointment today with the epilepsy nurse, Christina. This was pretty straightforward, so nothing really to report.

Melissa's breathing has worsened recently, and Angela managed to arrange a last-minute meeting with her while she was in seeing Christina. She commissioned an x-ray that showed what Angela suspected—a chylothorax. This is a pleural effusion with chyle. We all produce chyle but LAM prevents Melissa's body from getting rid of it. It has built up in her chest cavity causing the lung to squash and collapse. This explains the breathing deterioration.

We asked Angela if it is true that there is a life expectancy for a transplanted lung. She confirmed that there was, up to ten years. I don't know what I was expecting to hear, but this was not nice news. We still have hopes resting with the Rapamycin drug. There was good news on this front. Angela told us that Dr Pelgrum (kidney specialist) administers Rapamycin to some of his transplant patients, and therefore has access to this elusive drug. Finally, we have some usefulness from the renal team!

Melissa then went to Ward F6 for the insertion of a chest drain to remove the chylous fluid. The procedure went well and about 1800 ml of pink fluid (think mucus infused strawberry milkshake) poured out very quickly into the floor standing chamber.

X

FRIDAY, 11 JANUARY 2008

Melissa was in terrible pain this morning, and nurses seemed to ignore her for over an hour! It seems that the speed that the fluid came out probably caused Melissa's pain. In hindsight, the doctors would have liked to clamp it much earlier to prevent that much coming out so quickly. The speed in which the fluid came out caused the lung to fully inflate and hit the chest wall. This caused discomfort as the lung rubbed abrasively against the wall.

They administered morphine that stemmed the pain. The Pain Assessment Team came round to assess the situation and advised the doctors to keep going with morphine as it seemed to be working well.

The pain was not too bad, *but* the morphine had relaxed Melissa so much that she was hardly working her lungs. With LAM, obviously this was extremely dangerous, and Melissa was very close to respiratory failure. Angela came round to check on her progress and noticed how tiny Melissa's pupils were. She sent for some blood gases that showed carbon dioxide levels of 8 (should be 2-3, more like 3-4 in LAM patients). Emergency injections were dished out immediately to counteract the morphine. Melissa spent the night in intensive care. That was far too close for comfort.

Glad to see the pain doctors are on the ball.

x

SUNDAY, 13 JANUARY 2008

Melissa was given the all clear yesterday and was sent back to F6 ward. Everyone was expecting her to be discharged by now (including the doctors), but her oxygen levels are still not good. No one could really understand why her breathing was not any better after the chest drain. So she's staying in hospital. The drain is still pumping out chyle, much more than expected, about 1500 ml every twenty-four hours. There was talk of arranging a portable chest drain bag designed to catch the fluid in the same way as the floor-standing chamber. It has a valve so Melissa can empty it herself. This way Melissa could go home and give baby Miles some proper, valuable mummy love instead of being hooked up to a hospital bed with Miles just plonked at the foot end. However, they are now worried that the tube is being blocked too frequently due to calcium coming out within the chyle and causing sticky lumps in the tube. This needs flushing through frequently, and they are worried about infection if this was being flushed through at home.

There was also talk of putting a shunt in place to push the chyle away from the chest cavity into the abdomen. Some chyle would be absorbed in this process but probably too much would still remain.

There does not appear to be any real options at the moment.

x

TUESDAY, 15 JANUARY 2008

Okay, we have a plan. Angela has been working overtime as usual for us. We are now going for injecting some . . . wait for it . . . radioactive substance into the foot!! "Of course", I hear you say.

It is from the foot that the lymphatics operate. So the radioactive substance will be drawn up, and this substance can be traced with further x-rays. We can then, hopefully, conclude where the chyle is coming from. If it is coming from the chest itself, we can go for thoracic surgery—tying a knot in the thoracic duct—and if it is coming from the mass of cyst-type things in the area below the kidneys, we can think about removing them. Unfortunately, it could be coming from various areas, in which case it's back to the drawing board.

Well, we sort of missed Miles' 0 birthday. He was due to be born on 11 January 2008. I expect he is very glad he escaped from his mum's tummy in double-quick time!

x

THURSDAY, 17 JANUARY 2008

Well the radiologists decided that the injection should go through the hands. Melissa asked them if they were sure about this because Angela had specifically said feet. They continued with an injection between the fingers.

Angela spoke to Melissa this morning. The radiologists injected in the wrong place. So Melissa is now being sent down for an injection in the foot (tomorrow). Arghhhh. Between them, they think that it might have needed doing through the fingers too anyway. But *might* means *might not*. Anyway, the injection between the fingers did not show up any excess chyle being produced in the chest area. The injection between the toes will hopefully establish whether the bulk of production is from the abdomen or other areas. We are hoping it is not from lots of areas.

The chyle is taking a lot of protein and vitamins out of Melissa's body with it. This is becoming a major concern with Angela and today Melissa has started a wonderful diet. Basically, it consists of powder and water. Mmmmmm yummy.

It will build up protein and vitamins and has a complete lack of fat. Chyle is mainly produced with fat.

We are hoping this reduces the amount of chyle draining on a daily basis. Well, I am, I'm not too sure if Melissa wants this diet to work!?

Miles is a bit constipated at the moment, and he seems to be in pain, at times straining. We are giving a couple of ounces of cooled boiled water. Apparently, the Nutriprem 2 feed for premature babies is renowned for this.

MONDAY, 21 JANUARY 2008

Miles and I took the day off from being at the hospital yesterday. Unfortunately, Melissa does not have that option!

The results from the injection of radioactive substance between the toes show that there are no obvious areas producing this amount of chyle. Melissa is now glowing, and if you listen closely enough, you can hear her buzzing! All to no avail.

The diet has reduced the daily output of chyle. It's now 0.6 litre-1.0 litre daily. The consistency is thinner and less likely to block.

The tubes get blocked quite frequently and only doctors can flush them through. Finding a nurse, who then has to find a doctor, who then has to find the time to do this, can take a long while. In the meantime, chyle builds up in the lung, Melissa gets much shorter of breath, and when someone finally gets round to flushing, it rushes out quickly, causing pain too. It seems a constant battle when the drain needs flushing. The doctors are reluctant to do it more than once a day because of risk of infection.

So thinner is better, but Melissa is feeling very lightheaded when she gets up. In addition, the diet makes her feel quite sick from time to time. Angela has suggested supplementing the diet with add-on foods; these are to be fat free.

Miles is over nine pounds now, a little chubster. He is still constipated. The neonatal after-care nurse has advised us to give him a teaspoon of prune juice mixed with a teaspoon of cooled boiled water. Sounds explosive!

x

FRIDAY, 25 JANUARY 2008

Dr Pelgrum has got hold of the Rapamycin drug, and Melissa is now on it. This is great news. It won't help the chyle but will prevent the LAM getting worse and possibly reduce the size of some of the AMLs on her kidneys (and possibly reduce some of the cysts on her lungs).

Angela has told us that a possible direction for the chyle dilemma is for Mr Finn, chest surgeon, to do exploratory surgery. He will open up, have a look at the situation, and decide on the spot his course of action. This could include tying up the thoracic duct entirely. He will try to see Melissa while she's on the ward. This operation would be done at Papworth Hospital (about a twenty-minute drive from Addenbrookes).

Before any chest surgery is performed, the giant AML on the kidney must be dealt with. Angela is waiting to hear from the elusive Mr Dent who is the expert on kidney operations. He will have advice on whether it's best to remove the AML surgically or embolise the AML. As mentioned before, this is where the blood vessel supplying the AML is located, and a coil is inserted to prevent blood from feeding the AML. This would be done via the groin and would not involve open surgery.

We'll wait and see.

x

TUESDAY, 29 JANUARY 2008

Mr Dent has been found!! His opinion is to go for embolising the AML on Melissa's kidney.

This will be done on Friday, 1 February. It comes with sixty-forty chance of success. Not a great statistic really.

I was shown how to flush the chest drain through in a sterile way. Melissa hopes to come home after the embolisation before heading up to Papworth for the chest surgery scheduled for 12 February. So while she's at home, I'll need to flush her drain through when it is blocked. I'm not to do it more than once a day (even if it gets blocked again in the meantime) to reduce risk of infection. They are going with this principle at the moment at the hospital too. They might be better off putting some of the doctors on a refresher course on how to do the flush in a sterile way—some of them are clearly not well trained. This makes a mockery of the paranoia they have regarding infection.

We are looking forward to being together at home next week, even if Melissa stays in bed most of the time. It will mean Miles will get more attention and spend more time with Mummy and possibly even giving me some time to get on with other, relatively unimportant stuff.

x

FRIDAY, 1 FEBRUARY 2008

Melissa has had her AML embolised. The surgeon was very happy, so we are assuming it was successful. We need to give it a while before confirming success. Melissa seems okay. She probably didn't bat an eyelid! This procedure would have been nothing compared to what she has been through before.

Melissa's parents are looking after Miles tonight—I have a gig. They will keep hold of him tomorrow while I collect Melissa because discharge can be a nightmare to sort out—if I'm not chasing around, it could take most of the day.

x

SUNDAY, 3 FEBRUARY 2008

I forgot to say on the last post that Melissa has a CT scan lined up for Monday, and so she had to go back in this evening. We only got a one-day leave in the end!

This might seem a bit of a shame, but the reality of it is that Melissa and I are relieved. Friday night and yesterday saw Melissa develop a fever (a typical symptom of embolisation) and so being at home was difficult.

The diet that Melissa is on is hard enough without feeling rough, so she could not manage much of that. This will mean her albumen (protein) levels will drop—this is very low anyway and concerns Angela.

I flushed the drain to unblock it Saturday evening but (as usual) not much later that night it blocked up again. We had to wait until we returned to the hospital before it could get flushed again. In the meantime, the chyle built up inside Melissa's lungs, and she really started to struggle breathing. Also now, because the drain has been in so long, chyle is weeping out of the hole in Melissa's body where the drain enters. This made for a wet bed, wet clothes, and cold body. Not helpful when Melissa's going hot and cold with the fever anyway.

So we got back to hospital today and even though it took another four hours before someone could be bothered to actually tend to Melissa, flush the drain, and change the dressing, we were pretty relieved. Miles was dropped at Melissa's parents again, as I had a lunchtime gig in Cambridge with the originals band I'm involved in. When I got there, it was apparent that the gig was not going ahead—promoter notoriously unreliable. Very annoying—this difficult day could have been a whole lot easier if we knew the gig was not going ahead.

I hope Melissa gets a better night tonight.

I hope Miles doesn't mind being dropped off elsewhere all the time.

I hope I can ~~prevent my head from exploding~~ stay calm.

x

MONDAY, 4 FEBRUARY 2008

Melissa had a CT scan this morning. This was for comparison with the old CT scan. If the old CT scan showed the thoracic duct as being inflamed, and the new CT scan shows things in a more settled state, they could assume the inflammation was due to the pregnancy. All the information gathered from this might give more of a clue to the chest surgeon as to a course of action with the chest surgery.

Melissa is still feeling rough. She can't really face the crappy diet and although she is eating dry white fish, dry jacket potato, salad with no dressing, boiled chicken, etc., to supplement the diet, you get the feeling she really needs one of her mum's roast dinners to get her back on track.

If her albumen levels drop too much, she could be in for tube feeding. Yet another attachment to her body! If this does happen, she will not be allowed to eat anything through the mouth.

Angela is not in this week. This is not good news. She has always kept right on top of Melissa's condition and already by the end of today; we can notice a drop in the level of care. The fever has brought Melissa's infection risk to a high level, yet she hasn't had her observations monitored today. No one is keeping on top of her diet—she obviously can't do this stupid diet at the moment, but no one is arranging an alternative or at least talking to Melissa about resolving the issue. I think a lot of the nurses are scared of seeing to Melissa because of her rare condition and not being confident enough with the surprises it throws up.

Melissa has had enough (it took her long enough!). She is really quite low at the moment, which is understandable.

It goes without saying she will be an in-patient for the duration—until she gets transferred next week to Papworth Hospital for chest surgery.

x

TUESDAY, 5 FEBRUARY 2008

Miles weighs in at 11 pounds 5 ounces.
Fat boy!
x

FRIDAY, 8 FEBRUARY 2008

The chest drain was leaking this morning through a small hole. It needs to be removed and replaced. The doctors were amazed it lasted so long, but it is a shame it isn't going to last another few days until the chest operation is out the way. So it was clamped this morning.

The chest surgeon, Mr Finn, told us to both be around this morning, so he could talk to us about the operation. He did not show up this morning.

Melissa had an appointment at the hairdressers downstairs in the hospital (yes, in the hospital alongside a bank and travel agent!) at 14:00. This was something for her to look forward to this week, and Mr Finn had still not shown. We let the ward sister know, and Melissa went down for her hair appointment anyway. You can guess what happened—Mr Finn came round to see Melissa! Melissa was called back up to the ward, so she's got half a cut. Melissa is not bothered about this. It will take a lot to get her fazed at the moment, especially in connection with her image or other such trivial things.

So, the meeting. It's not a rosy picture by any means. The procedure is to make two or three small openings in Melissa's right side to get into the lung area. Then they will deflate the right lung, so Mr Finn can access the thoracic duct. If the lung is stuck to the chest wall, he will need to make the three holes into one big hole so as to get access with as little messing around with the lung as possible. In Melissa's case, the lungs are very fragile. This type of operation comes with a 60 percent to 70 percent success rate. Mr Finn has not done this procedure with a LAM patient before. If successful, he still is not sure if the chyle will build up in a different area—possibly in the stomach or legs. Previously, in patients for whom he has tied up the thoracic duct, the chyle has been absorbed, but LAM can affect the lymphatic system in strange ways, so he is unsure.

All in all, not much of a success rate and even success could mean problems elsewhere. Surgeons do tend to paint the worst possible picture though.

Melissa has looked better over the last couple of days. This is because she has stopped that stupid diet—it was making her throw up in the end. They have now decided to stick a tube through the nose and into the gut. This will ensure her protein levels are up, and she's in good shape for the op. A nurse came round and tried to stick this tube up Melissa's nose—but after the fourth attempt and a bit of vomiting, she decided to ask someone else to do it.

So the dietician sister came and did his best. He fought through the projectile vomiting and eventually got the tube in. Persistent! As you can imagine, Melissa's throat felt a little ripped up at this point.

Later on, Melissa threw up again, and brought half the tube out with it. The nurse had to take it out. So after all that, we are back to square one. In fact, worse off—the food that Melissa ate has been brought up and therefore any chance of building up her albumen squandered. She feels more comfortable without the tube in though.

x

Saturday, 9 February 2008

They're taping up the hole in the chest drain tube—this means they won't need to put a new hole in Melissa. Bonus!
x

MONDAY, 11 FEBRUARY 2008

A skin infection has developed around the site where the drain enters. This is very painful for Melissa. They are leaving it until Melissa gets to Papworth where they will give her antibiotics after the op anyway.

Melissa was transferred to Papworth at about 17:00. We were in the posh end—private! The side room was a bit like a hotel room. Well, it was compared to F6 ward at Addenbrookes anyway. We were on Varrier Jones Ward.

Melissa needed pain relief but had to wait for a drug chart to be written up by a doctor before she could be given any.

The chest drain (surprise, surprise) was blocked. A sister came in to see Melissa and asked, "So what am I expected to do with this?" She looked down at the chamber and blocked tube that drained from Melissa's chest. This did not fill us with confidence.

The doctor came in to write up a drug chart. The notes received from Addenbrookes were apparently all over the place. He had spent quite a bit of time sorting through them. He wrote up a drugs chart. Incorrectly. There was no pain relief written down. The epilepsy medication was written down for morning, but the evening tablet was not written down. Our confidence dropped again. Melissa, in the meantime, was still not getting any painkillers. The doctor went back to his desk to try again.

We decided that if Melissa could deal with the breathlessness associated with a blocked chest drain, and with the build up of chyle inside the chest cavity, it would be better to leave it than getting one of this lot to flush it through to unblock it.

I left, quite late, with Melissa still not getting any sort of pain relief.

TUESDAY, 12 FEBRUARY 2008

Melissa did not get the drain flushed and held out. In fact, the drain unblocked itself slightly and a bit of chyle trickled through overnight so that helped.

All set for surgery then. She left her side room at 09:30. On the way down, the side arm of her bed dropped and knocked the tub of chyle flying, tugging on the infected site as it dropped. Ouch. That must have really hurt, although I didn't hear Melissa scream. Chyle was spilled all over the floor. What a mess. Great start!

I waited in the side room . . . and waited and waited and waited. At 13:30, a nurse came in to get Melissa's hearing aids. She did not know anything about how Melissa was. I was left to assume that she was now in recovery. I could not visit her.

At 16:00, I got a message from a nurse that Melissa was okay. It was nice to hear something six and a half hours after Melissa had left the room—but this was somewhat limited information.

I decided to head over to recovery without asking. I got to the door and buzzed. Mr Finn came out to see me. He explained that he had to make a slightly bigger incision than he would have hoped. Also, the thoracic duct was abnormally swollen. As a result, it was stuck to the gullet. Therefore, he had to manipulate the gullet quite a lot. This meant that Melissa could be "Nil By Mouth" for a couple of days. For those who don't recognise this hospital phrase this means no food or drink could pass Melissa's lips.

On a very positive side of things, he was pleased that he saw a definite leak from a particular area of the thoracic duct. He tied that bit up as well as the top and the bottom of the duct. He also clamped up a few other dubious areas.

At 17:00, I was given permission to go and see Melissa in Recovery. She looked pretty beaten up, as to be expected. The surgeon's assistant had really botched up putting a line in to the back of Melissa's hand—apparently blood had been spurting out everywhere.

The nurses in recovery were very rough with Melissa, and she was quite upset when I saw her. She told me that they had told her, "You don't have to cry." What a nasty thing to say! Melissa was in an awful lot of pain. They had her on morphine. Morphine had previously caused Melissa to come close to respiratory failure, and this made us nervous. We were constantly telling every new face we saw about this.

Melissa was then transferred back to the ward. The catheter had not been put in properly and needed putting in again, and this was done in a clumsy way. So, a bit of a wet bed. Melissa was not feeling any effect from the morphine. We then saw a leak from the line that the surgeon's assistant had cocked up, through which the morphine was injected. We could see that the bung on the side had not been screwed on properly and told the nurse who was getting more and more stressed. She wasn't really listening properly and proceeded to undo the dressing and have a good investigation of where the line entered the skin. She looked up at us and said, "It all looks fine to me", as though the wet mess around the site was irrelevant. We pointed out that the bung was not screwed on properly, again. Then the penny dropped.

Melissa was still in a lot of pain, and no one was taking any notice. The hand was quite swollen, and eventually they thought they would flush it through. It was totally blocked, and the injected saline burst into Melissa very forcefully when it unblocked—ouch. So for the previous six or so hours Melissa had not been getting any painkillers. No painkillers after a major operation into her chest. It is hard for me to imagine the pain Melissa has had to bear over the last few years; I feel humbled by her but also so desperately sorry for her.

She was taken back to critical care. She was injected with a spinal block and had one-on-one care. I felt a bit happier and left Melissa at 01:00. I went back to collect my things to discover they were all gathered up and turfed out of the room. I had to go into an office and sign papers and discuss what valuables are being left in the office, etc. I really did not need to go through that after today's events. The drive home was in extreme fog, so I couldn't go any faster than 30 mph. I was shattered.

Overnight Melissa had her line removed, as it was not looking good. They did not put another one in until four hours later. The pain was intense again, and no one was looking after her. One doctor in a hurry moaned he had thirty-two other patients to look at. Good for him. I thought she had one-on-one care?

Melissa finally got to sleep at 07:00. She was woken at 08:00. This was not the way we were expecting Melissa's road to recovery to go.

x

WEDNESDAY, 13 FEBRUARY 2008

Today Melissa has got a good carer—hoorah! Kiera is a pain nurse who is doing a great job of making Melissa feel a bit calmer, steadier, and generally better.

The physiotherapist is happy with progress—doing on the spot marching and breathing exercises.

Melissa started to drink a little water. Fortijuice is fed through a tube—100 mm every hour. Medication was kept down. Melissa would be out of critical care now, but there is no bed elsewhere.

The staff in Critical Care were all a little perturbed by me bringing Miles in with me. I can understand that, but we are supposed to be parents! It looks like we should get away with it.

x

THURSDAY, 14 FEBRUARY 2008

The NG tube used to feed through the nose is giving my valentine a swollen throat and ear pain. She would rather have a TPN tube (a tube that's inserted into the chest) than the nose thing.

Melissa was transferred back to Varrier Jones Ward at 12:00. Kim is Melissa's nurse for the day. She's good.

I left early for a gig. Miles got dropped off at Melissa's mum and dad's again!

x

FRIDAY, 15 FEBRUARY 2008

Mr Finn is in danger from Melissa's mum. The sight of him sends her weak at the knees!

He came round and was pleased with the progress. He was happy that Melissa is keeping down water and tube feeds. He wants to put a good feed into the tube by drip so that Melissa doesn't get woken throughout the night. He's going to try a glass of milk on Monday!

Melissa is looking a lot better today. She's managed to get out of the gown and into some clothes. She is breathing easier than she has done in a long time.

x

MONDAY, 18 FEBRUARY 2008

Over the weekend, Melissa has developed what appears to be an infection affecting her ears and throat. Her breathing has really deteriorated. This might be due to the infection but could more likely be blood clots. Melissa is coughing up blood and because her temperature is not high, it is thought there are blood clots in and around the lungs. A CT scan tomorrow should give a clearer picture.

Melissa had a glass of milk this morning, and Mr Finn was very pleased that nothing came out of the chest drain after that. He said to carry on drinking milk and anything else she liked orally. If all goes well, he will take the chest drain and NG tube out.

x

TUESDAY, 19 FEBRUARY 2008

The CT scan results showed a small infection on the chest. IV antibiotics were administered.

Melissa's breathing is still bad. She is still coughing up what we assume are clots of blood. She now has an injection in her tummy once a day to thin the blood.

Is this real? We were hoping this horrible operation would help Melissa's breathing.

x

THURSDAY, 21 FEBRUARY 2008

Not much has changed. There is talk of Melissa being transferred back to Addenbrookes.

Getting home seems harder than a prison escape. Not that we think that's where Melissa should be right now.

x

P.S. Miles is now 13 pounds 12 ounces. Piling it on. I had him weighed by our health visitors at the medical centre on my way in. He is off the graph, and they were telling me I should watch what he eats and try and get his weight controlled and within the lines on the graph. They can f*** off and realise there are more important issues than the chubbiness of a four-month-old baby, who was born over ten weeks early by the way. Arghhh!

FRIDAY, 22 FEBRUARY 2008

Melissa has been transferred to Addenbrookes. At least we'll get to see Angela—that's always worthwhile.

One of the doctors came and said that after conversing with Papworth, they now consider Melissa's breathing problem to be mainly due to pneumonia. They are still not ruling out blood clots. The pneumonia will be treated with IV antibiotics. Melissa was already taking these so at least the course has already started.

Melissa's breathing is terrible. Going to the toilet is very difficult even with oxygen. She has to use a commode instead at the moment.

No sign of Angela.

x

TUESDAY, 26 FEBRUARY 2008

Melissa has been released! Over the last few days, the pneumonia diagnosis has been confirmed, and clots ruled out. Melissa has slightly improved, and this is why she can get home. It is treatable at home with tablet-form antibiotics, but she will have to properly rest.

We have planned for her to stay at her parents' house where there is a downstairs toilet and assistance in abundance!

Angela came round and agreed this was an excellent idea. She was amazed and very pleased that Melissa coped with one lung (supported with a ventilator) during the operation.

The open surgery ventilator is a procedure that comes with risk of Hospital Pneumonia.

We got to Melissa's parents' house quite late and had a lovely dinner with the family before going to bed—our room had Melissa, Miles, Karma (our dog), and myself. It's like a dream has come true!

X

WEDNESDAY, 27 FEBRUARY 2008

Melissa is trying to do too much! Does this come as a surprise to anyone?!

x

FRIDAY, 29 FEBRUARY 2008

Melissa has had a change of heart and has taken it nice and easy—mainly lying in bed upstairs. She has made nice progress this way. More of the same required.

x

TUESDAY, 4 MARCH 2008

More steady progress, but it will take some time to get rid of this pneumonia.

Miles is still constipated! He takes lactolose and cooled boiled water to no avail. It doesn't stop him being an absolute treasure.

x

TUESDAY, 11 MARCH 2008

Miles went to see the pediatrician today. Dr Warnock was very happy with his progress and after putting the little chap through his paces, he said that he was catching up quite quickly. In fact, he is behaving like a twelve-week-old, halfway between his birthday and due date. It usually takes two years to catch up, so this is looking fairly quick.

He recommended we change milk from the Nutriprem 2 to First Stage Baby Milk to ease the constipation. Perhaps having a go at feeding fruit and veg at some point—if he takes it great, if not maybe later.

Another appointment will be made for three months from now.

Good boy!!

x

WEDNESDAY, 12 MARCH 2008

Melissa's breathing has got a lot worse over the last few days, and when we reported the saturation levels to Professor Wendall over the phone, he arranged an immediate x-ray. After the x-ray, we got to see Professor Wendall (Angela is away), and he explained that although the pneumonia appears to have gone, the dreaded chyle was back to haunt us.

This time it has built up on the other lung (Melissa's left). The thoracic duct was successfully tied up, but the chyle could have got in through a burst cyst on the lung. Unbelievable. We now just expect this disease to constantly throw up horrors for Melissa to try and deal with while the experts try to figure out ways of fixing or relieving the issues. Melissa was admitted into Ward F6 again. Home from home.

She had a chest drain inserted quite low and in a fairly awkward place to get maximum benefit (but cause maximum pain!). Chyle started coming out and was stopped at 150 ml.

Later the valve on the drain was opened up again and after three minutes, there was 700 ml in the container. We stopped it at that point, as it was very painful.

Another x-ray determined that the drain was in the correct place, and the lung was looking fairly empty on the chyle front. However, Melissa's breathing is not much better, which is hard to fathom.

The transplant expert is being asked to see Melissa for advice on any action that may be needed. To eliminate chyle entering the left lung, the lung can be stuck to the chest wall so that there is no cavity, but this could affect Melissa's chances of being okayed for transplant. A discussion is required.

Well, she had three weeks at home. What more can we ask for?!

x

SATURDAY, 15 MARCH 2008

Melissa's drain has removed a total of 1800 ml so far but appears to have stopped draining now. The doctors are flushing it through tonight, and if no more than 100 ml drains over the next twenty-four hours or so, the tube is coming out, and Melissa will be let out again.

If the leak is continuous as before, then it appears there are three options:

1. Pleurodesis—through existing drain, talc is pushed through the tube into the chest cavity to stick the lung to the chest wall. This prevents there being a cavity.

2. Pleurodesis—surgically with general anaesthetic to achieve the same result. This way is more invasive, but we assume it does a better job. Having said that, a better job might not be desired as lung transplant would become more difficult.

3. Portable bag with a permanent tube in the chest cavity—draining chyle. Worn like a handbag!

Now is the right time for transplant assessment. Information, scans, history, etc., of lungs, kidneys, lymphatic system are all being gathered together at the moment.

We need to decide where Melissa would want the transplant, Papworth Hospital or Newcastle's Freeman Hospital.

Professor Wendall wants to get an assessment sorted out within a week or two. He seems to think a transplant will happen pretty soon, assessment permitting. Is this telling us that Melissa has not got long left as things stand?

At Papworth Hospital, 75 percent to 80 percent of lung transplant patients survive beyond the dreaded first six months.

These statistics (like the one about five- to ten-year lifespan) apply to all lung transplants. LAM patients generally have a slightly better outlook because they are usually much younger patients. Papworth has been known to refuse lung transplants for patients who have had a pleurodesis. Papworth is only forty minutes away—Miles doesn't mind this journey.

Freeman Hospital has Dr Holmes who is spoken of as the best in the business. They perform the most lung transplants each year in the UK by far and have the best reputation. As a result, they have the most patients on their waiting list—more than the amount of lungs they are allocated, so waiting times could be longer. On the LAM foundation forum, the people on there with LAM have nothing but good things to say about Freeman. Of lung transplant patients at Freeman, 85 percent survive beyond the dreaded first six months. The team at Freeman Hospital are happy to operate after a pleurodesis. Newcastle is a five-hour drive—I'm not sure if Miles would like that so much!

Our initial thoughts are Freeman, whatever the cost and mileage. They have transplanted seven LAM patients. Papworth has done one or two. In addition, we've seen what the care is like at Papworth first hand, and bar one or two nurses, it was not good at all.

We need to sleep on all this information. Although neither of us slept well last night for various reasons.

Miles has been quite irritable over the last day or so, and he must have only got three or four hours sleep last night—next to me as he would not have it in his cot. I've not really seen him cry like that yet but maybe that just shows how good he's been. He's done two poos today though and seems a bit better. I hope that it was just that and not something more awkward.

SUNDAY, 16 MARCH 2008

Melissa's breathlessness is probably due to the fact that the lung was deflated for a long while and is taking time to "un-crumble."

We had the good news that the drain was going to come out this morning. The weekend doctor came round and pulled it out only to witness that chyle started to pour out of the hole that the tube had left in Melissa's back. The doctor decided, eventually, that the wound needed stitching up. She temporarily patched up the hole and went off to prepare the treatment room.

We wheeled over to the treatment room and, as the temporary dressing was removed, out came the chyle again. I suggested letting the chyle come out before stitching up the hole. I held a sick bowl below the wound and caught chyle that was spurting out of Melissa's back. The doctor decided to stitch up the hole after about 500 ml came out.

Basically, the hole is now sealed but we don't know what the hell is going on. It would not surprise us if another drain will be required pretty soon. Melissa will have an x-ray later today. Melissa is fed up with these drains and will probably scream at the next person who suggests another one should go in.

We can't wait for the lung transplant now. We never thought we'd be saying that. We have chosen the Freeman Hospital to be our saviour.

Miles had his first feed on solids today. Parsnip, straight from Bob's allotment. He wasn't gulping it down by any means, but he was still eating it!

x

TUESDAY, 18 MARCH 2008

Melissa thinks that chyle is building up again, but her breathing is not too bad at the moment. We need to bear in mind when Melissa's breathing is very good; it is comparable to you and I breathing through a small straw with shallow breaths. She will have a chest x-ray today (they couldn't fit it in yesterday) and will also tie up any remaining reports and tests to finish compiling the information required for transplant assessment.

We are hoping the x-ray will not show much chyle. They may even poke a long needle into the lung to syringe out the chyle for now!!

Professor Wendall is contacting Freeman Hospital today and hopes to get a quick response as to if and when they would like Melissa to see them.

Melissa has reduced her oxygen intake through the mask from 35 percent (at 8 litres/minute) to 28 percent (at 4 litres/minute) so that if we get home, we are comfortable with the oxygenator that can only provide a maximum of 5 litres/minute. Her saturation levels are 86 percent so that's pretty good for her.

x

WEDNESDAY, 19 MARCH 2008

Melissa is home!

The x-ray showed a little chyle but not enough to concern them too much. The registrar had to complete a report that took some time. This was the last of the information Newcastle need in preparation for assessment with exception of a bone density scan that has been booked in for two weeks time.

Melissa is still really struggling to move around though and has to really take her time. We've just bought a wheelchair off eBay— we could always sell it once the transplant is done.

It's nice to have the family back together. Let's hope it lasts a bit longer this time.

x

THURSDAY, 20 MARCH 2008

Well that didn't last very long. Melissa got home at 15:00 yesterday, and we were back in hospital at 10:00 this morning.

It is not easy getting about. Although the wheelchair helps, it is still a challenge with Melissa on the wheelchair, Miles on Melissa's lap, an oxygen tank hanging over the handlebars, a rucksack containing nappies and food for Miles on my back, a bag of things for Miles to play with on the end of one arm and, of course, hands on the wheelchair.

Her breathing was really bad last night and trying to get up the stairs was scary to say the least. Melissa's heart was pounding trying to get oxygen around the body.

We just drove to Addenbrookes this morning without appointment and are back on F6 with a new chest drain. Yep, the x-ray showed another build up of chyle.

The pneumonia has really damaged Melissa's lungs, and the consensus is that there is little chance of Melissa's breathing getting back to how it was just after the chest operation at Papworth, before the pneumonia kicked in. It is such a shame that the difficult and risky operation to tie up the thoracic duct in Melissa's chest was successful but totally spoilt by the hospital pneumonia.

We are resigned to the fact that Melissa will struggle to get to and from the toilet until she has a transplant.

It seems that one of the AMLs on Melissa's kidneys has burst again. Not as bad as the last time, so we are hoping that it is a small one.

Easter weekend starts tomorrow, so we won't really have any news until Tuesday. Between the doctors here at Addenbrookes, the surgeons at the Freeman, and ourselves, we will work out what the best course of action is for now, until the assessment. If the chyle continues to come out (very likely, even if it is a lot slower than before) then is Melissa going to use the portable chest drain or have a pleurodesis? We shall see.

Miles is a growing lad.

x

MONDAY, 31 MARCH 2008

Melissa remains in the hospital, although she did get leave to attend a friend's funeral last Thursday and more leave to attend a friend's leaving do on Saturday. Both these events involved going down to the pub and drinking wine. This worried me sick; she had oxygen tanks with a tube into her nostrils and a portable bag collecting chyle via a tube into her lungs, and she's in a pub! In fairness, she did not feel too bad the next days.

Yesterday's check of chyle discharge quantity over twenty-four hours is up by quite a lot to what it has been. I hope that this is not a trend.

The Freeman Hospital has decided against a pleurodesis now as it will probably be too much for Melissa's lungs to deal with. What on earth are Melissa's lungs like now?

The drain will probably remain in place. She is to go on a low-fat diet until she sees Newcastle for transplant assessment, which unless she gets an earlier cancellation is now booked in for Monday, 14 April.

There is some sort of injection just under the skin that Angela wants to try. On other patients who produce chyle, this either stopped the production entirely, stopped it temporarily, limited, it or didn't affect it. It has not been used on a LAM patient yet, but it's worth a go.

Miles is five months old tomorrow. He looks like he's got conjunctivitis and is showing some signs of teething, so he's not his usual smiley, happy self at the moment, but he's coping with it all pretty well. I'm sure he knows the way to and from Addenbrookes by now.

THURSDAY, 3 APRIL 2008

The chyle discharge quantity has been much less recently. It just seems every now and then there is a large quantity.

Melissa came home today. We won't get our hopes up, but the plan is to stay home until our visit to Newcastle. She seems to be doing well. I am doing the nurse things such as changing the drain tub/bag, changing the dressing and flushing the drain through. I must get a uniform . . .

Miles has almost recovered from the conjunctivitis but now has a lingering cough that annoys him. He's chatting in "a-goo's" quite a lot now. Ahhhh.

x

FRIDAY, 4 APRIL 2008

Back to Addenbrookes! But Melissa is okay.

Now Miles, not to be out-done by his mother, has a nasal cannula for oxygen and a feed tube going up his nose and is on C3 Ward.

His cough continued, and he started to miss a couple of his feeds. As we all know, Miles enjoys his food, so this was not a good sign! We saw our GP in the afternoon and, after a listen to his chest, he immediately spoke to Addenbrookes and referred him. Then he called in his colleague for a listen on Miles' chest. This prompted us to ask if Miles chest was particularly strange sounding.

"It is unusual; I think he has an infection at the top part of his lungs," was the response.

We do not like the word unusual anymore.

Off we went to A+E at Addenbrookes. Again. Miles' temperature was rising by the minute, and he was burning up by the time he was seen. Bloods were okay, but x-ray showed a spot of pneumonia. PNEUMONIA?! He was to be given IV antibiotics—but getting a line in to Miles' veins proved quite difficult. In fact, after trying both wrists and both feet, the registrar decided to leave it for the night doctor.

In the meantime, Miles was moved to C3 Ward, and we settled in.

I was getting a distinct feeling of déjà-vu, except Melissa refused to settle down in the buggy.

Miles is to be kept in overnight.

x

SATURDAY, 5 APRIL 2008

We phoned up the hospital this morning and managed to speak with a pediatrician who told us that Miles probably has bronchiolitis, possibly pneumonia too. The treatment remains the same. He actually has a partial lung collapse! This sounds worse than it is apparently. A small pocket of mucus has got trapped in the lung. When the mucus goes, the lung will re-expand.

We got up to the hospital late morning. He still managed a few smiles and a little bit of a chat this afternoon. He is now asleep. To be honest, apart from the occasional cough and requiring a bit more comforting than usual, he appears on the surface to be okay.

When the oxygen is not firing up his nose, his saturation levels are not great though—down to 91 percent. This should be 98 percent minimum.

x

MONDAY, 7 APRIL 2008

The test results came back yesterday from the mucus samples, and Miles has Rhinovirus and Power Influenza. The IV antibiotics remained the same—a good all rounder apparently! That course finished today. An oral form of antibiotics continues. He is down to 0.25 litres/minute oxygen and has started bottle-feeding again. The NG tube has been removed as he has held down the bottle feeds so far today.

There was a lady on a bed opposite Melissa on Ward F6 with Rhinovirus, and she was with Miles for a while. It has hit home that a hospital is not the ideal place to bring up a baby.

He was smiling and chatting for quite a lot of today. He seems pretty healthy on the outside. His insides are coming out at quite a rate at the other end! This is part of the virus' side effects. So at least we've found a solution to his constipation.

We are hoping he will be home Wednesday. Fingers crossed . . .

X

TUESDAY, 8 APRIL 2008

Rapid recovery! Miles is off oxygen aids. The NG tube is out, and he is taking bottle feeds as and when he likes. And . . . HE IS BEING DISCHARGED!

Superb! The family returns. Again.

Poor old Miles still has a wheezy chest and is still a bit groggy but is generally looking great (by comparison). We have some oral antibiotics for him. His stomach is managing small feeds every three hours or so, and we're sure he'll soon be managing his usual amount every four hours or so.

What's next we wonder?

x

SUNDAY, 13 APRIL 2008

Miles has recovered totally now. It's fantastic to have him back, but the family splits up again tomorrow as Melissa and I are heading up to Newcastle for the transplant assessment. We're looking forward to it (not deserting Miles, tut).

x

FRIDAY, 18 APRIL 2008

We have just come back from four days at the Freeman Hospital, Newcastle for Melissa's lung transplant assessment.

It went very well. The train journey was quick (just under three hours) and the disabled assistance second to none—staff were ready at each station waiting at the right carriage with a ramp for us and helped with luggage to and from taxis. We were impressed, and it made the whole journey very easy.

The clinicians at the Freeman are fantastic. We got on very well with one of the transplant coordinators, George Graveson. He was very much on our level, extremely informative, realistic, and positive all in one!

Professor Bridges was to the point but still friendly. The surgeon, Mr Holmes, was happy to discuss things and was comfortable with Melissa's condition. We also had chats with physio and social services.

The four days was full of heavy information that left us feeling nervous, scared, and worried but also excited, relieved, and positive.

The bottom line is that Melissa has been put on the "active waiting list" for single left, single right, and double lung transplant. There is only one list, but we get the feeling Melissa is pretty high on the list. It helps that all options are open (single both sides *and* double) so every lung that passes the test (blood group, size, health, condition, etc.) will be a candidate for Melissa. It also helps that George understands our situation (Melissa is young and otherwise healthy, we have a baby boy). He keeps an idea in his mind of who would benefit most from the newly donated lung(s).

The main concerns are:

1. The scary statistics. Eighty-five percent of patients make it through the op and beyond the initial six months post op, 50 percent make it to five years, 35 percent to ten years (Prof. Bridges actually suggested that was now up to 40 percent).

2. The self-maintenance. While we wait, bags packed and by the door, for the call, Melissa must remain in good health. If she gets a cold or a cough, she must immediately inform George and will most likely be suspended from the list until she is over it. This could lead to missed calls. This is all due to the anti-rejection drugs. They will be administered at a massive dose once the newly donated lungs are in place to start with, and this will bring Melissa's immune system to a halt.

3. Post op risks. Obviously, when Melissa's immune system is at such a low, there is huge risk of infection that could prove fatal. Only two people (the same two people) are permitted to visit Melissa while she is in Intensive Care, and hygiene is imperative. Miles will certainly not be allowed anywhere near! Water will be purified, etc. After three weeks, the anti-rejection drugs can be reduced, and Melissa will be living in digs within the hospital grounds while she is under a watchful eye and attending rehabilitation programs at the gym. During this time, bronchoscopies are performed to ensure there are no signs of infection or rejection. There is a fine balance between getting it right with the anti-rejection drugs to cope with rejection and yet not attract infection.

The whole procedure is absolutely amazing. While Melissa is travelling up to Newcastle in an ambulance, a transplant coordinator is flying over to assess the donated lungs, flushing them through, and if they are good enough, storing them in ice and flying them back to Newcastle. By which time, Melissa will be in theatre clobber ready and waiting for the final check over of the lungs once landed. If the lungs are assessed as being no good before the need to fly them back to Newcastle, or after transit for that matter, the ambulance turns around, and Melissa comes back home, hopes dashed! This can be a harrowing experience. Especially if it happens on several occasions.

The chyle draining from Melissa's left lung seems to be lessening to a certain extent. I suppose there is an average of only about 200-300 ml daily discharging.

The Octreotide injections that Angela wanted to try have been obtained. Unfortunately, Melissa will be an in-patient at Addenbrookes for a few days (four or five) while these are administered so that she can be monitored closely. As the folks from Australia are coming over soon, we are hoping to get Melissa in tomorrow or Wednesday to get it over and done with. This is all a bit of a pain but could just turn out to be the best thing to happen to Melissa this year!

We're back home now, and it's great to see Miles. His grandparents have done a marvellous job; we've taken notes!

x

MONDAY, 28 APRIL 2008

Melissa has been in Addenbrookes trying out these injections to prevent the chyle leak. She was admitted last Thursday and should be home tomorrow. She is having three injections of Octreotide into the stomach just under the skin each day.

We don't want to get our hopes up too much, but it does appear to be slowing the chyle discharge right down. Melissa didn't drain anything over the first twenty-four hours, only 60 ml drained over the next twenty-four hours and 60 ml again the following day. It was between 200 ml and 400 ml each day before, so this is great news.

If it continues to work, there is talk of this injection eventually being reduced to once every month.

Miles is trying hard to sit up. He slept from seven at night through to six in the morning yesterday! Lovely.

x

Thursday, 1 May 2008

Melissa is coming home tomorrow. The Octreotide injections initially appeared to be working, but the chyle has been coming out at 150 ml to 200 ml again over the last couple of days. It was agreed that Melissa may as well go home to finish the fortnight course of injections.

At one point, they were contemplating taking the chest drain out, but the chyle started building up again. There was a cock up on the third day with one of the injections being missed (the wrong dose was sent up, and nothing was done about it) and this may have affected the way things have developed.

So because the drain remains in, Melissa can come home and continue the course at home. We are scheduled to go back to see Angela at her clinic next Thursday.

Miles has been enjoying his Aussie grandparents over the last couple of days. He's getting nicely comfortable with them! They have flown over to be with us for a couple of weeks.

x

My parents left for Oz this morning. They're stopping at Singapore for a few days to break up the journey and see somewhere new. It was lovely having them over, for all three of us. They'll be missed!

The Octreotide injections stopped a day or so early as it became obvious it was not working. We saw Angela last Thursday, and she was visibly disappointed too. That was the last throw of the dice, apart from Melissa being fed by drip through yet another chest tube. This would be to ensure Melissa intakes no fat whatsoever and gets all the nutrients required. Luckily, this plan was not really discussed, and we are back at Melissa's parents.

There is a stair lift on its way to our house (being fitted tomorrow) and, provided Melissa's respiratory nurse can organise two further oxygen concentrator machines that can stay there (so that we can leave the ones we have at Melissa's parents), we can head home and try to lead some form of normal life!! It will be a bit of an experiment because we do get a lot of help living at Chris and Frank's, so we'll just see how it goes.

Melissa needs two oxygen concentrator machines daisy-chained together now to double the output of the oxygen flow rate. She uses a mask more often than the nasal canula as the output is too forceful up the nose through a nasal canula to bear after a while.

We had a meeting with King's College Hospital to resolve the issues we have them. It was the end to an ongoing complaint about the way the doctors there knew Melissa had TSC but never informed Melissa. Knowledge of this may have changed our life's course. It would have most likely meant Melissa would not be in the state she is in now. LAM would have been diagnosed much sooner, and we would have been advised against pregnancy. It appears the pregnancy progressed Melissa's LAM from being a mild-to-moderate form into a severe form.

The meeting went well—it was all quite civilised with no one getting too hot headed (Melissa), and all points raised were dealt with. The doctors and chairlady were full of apologies and sympathy. The neurologist admitted he should have arranged a follow-up meeting just after surgery, as well as a further meeting several weeks after (with the surgeon in attendance). He also admitted that all action seemed to inexplicably stop, even though he had written in the notes to arrange a meeting with a geneticist to discuss TSC and how to inform Melissa and discuss her future, including referral to all other specialists necessary to keep a check on all other symptoms. That meeting with the geneticist never happened nor any meeting with Melissa.

It seemed to get everything off our chest. It was good for us that they could see exactly how Melissa is now and exactly what hell she has been through in the last year. They were all visibly shocked. They explained how their system has changed and will continue to change to improve. They believe a nurse should be involved with each patient to have more contact and keep consultants notes marrying up so nothing gets missed.

They are also speaking to the chief executive to see if they are able to offer any financial help. This would be nice as it was pointed out that Melissa has had to stop work, and I cannot find time to keep on top of finding work for myself.

Miles is doing really well, although the heat seems to knock him out a bit. Teething continues, and he goes through very uncomfortable patches, but you get the feeling worse is to come! He's chatting away to himself at the moment, fiddling about with a teether. It doesn't seem to be going near his mouth though!

x

MONDAY, 26 MAY 2008

We have a stair lift installed at home—courtesy of Daddy and brother Arnold. Thank you so much.

We managed to arrange for the delivery of two oxygen concentrators at home.

This all means that we are now living at home. We miss the company and help but at the same time, we gain independence, and there's nothing like home! It's a bit peaceful now but pretty hectic too?!

Melissa can take Miles up and down the stairs on her lap.

We are very jumpy when the phone goes—especially evening calls. Our bags are packed, and we are ready to go. The only difficulty with a sharp exit into an ambulance, should the call for

transplant come, will be arranging someone to babysit Miles until his nan and granddad get over to collect him. We'll deal with that at the time.

Miles is doing very well. I think he'll be a drummer—I had best go and buy a drum kit then!

x

FRIDAY, 27 JUNE 2008

Well it's a long overdue post, but that's mainly due to nothing major to report really.

We are still waiting for the transplant call. This is keeping us on our toes. It's a scary thought but at the same time, we want this operation to happen sooner rather than later.

There is some exciting news on the chyle leak front—it seems to have dried up! It's certainly not coming out of the chest drain anymore and hasn't been for the last week really. The drain has remained in but has been clamped, so there is no drainage chamber and tubing attached to Melissa any more. This has made her life a lot easier as you can imagine.

Liquid oxygen has now been installed. This is the newest addition to our oxygen station in a corner of our lounge. We now have two electric oxygen concentrators that Melissa uses throughout the night (giving her a flow rate of 8 litres per minute) and the new addition Mother Liquid Oxygen Unit giving options during the day. You can use the tap directly from the mother unit or use the mother tank to fill a portable unit up. It gives us a quiet option! Just don't bring a lighter into our house.

Miles is doing really well, as ever. He's a happy soul, looking to stand before he can sit let alone crawl! Probably because his belly gets in the way of the whole crawling thing.

We've managed to get out a bit recently. It was a bit of stress and a few arguments but quite nice to get some social life back.

I'll try and update quicker next time.

x

MONDAY, 28 JULY 2008

Melissa had her chest drain entirely removed a week ago! We had stopped the flow with the valve for a couple of weeks, opening up to drain once or twice in this period. Nothing was draining, and it appeared no chyle was building up in the chest cavity. The bold step was taken to remove the drain, and thankfully, it has proved that there is no build up of chyle going on.

This doesn't really mean that Melissa is suddenly in better condition, but it does mean that she feels a lot more confident—Melissa was always worried that the chest drain would catch on something and with dogs around that was always a possibility. In addition, this means there is one less thing to carry around, so things are logistically easier too.

Her breathing might have been a little better, but the weather has probably countered that.

It also means I can forget about the nurse duties!

Melissa asked again the dreaded question. She was told that she perhaps had a year left. We didn't query that we were told that back in February. We were just pleased with what we heard.

We have been receiving updates from a few LAM patients and their lung transplants. There are quite a few people with LAM using a kind of LAM forum via an email system that Melissa can access. It seems that everyone's road to recovery is very different, and even a successful recovery seems very likely to undergo a few scares along the way. We haven't heard of one going terribly wrong, but it is definitely not an easy ride. Not just a matter of "there's your new life, off you go." It's a very useful and comforting chat line for Melissa.

Miles is doing really well. He had a check over for early signs of Tuberous Sclerosis the other day and nothing suggests he has it. The results came back from Melissa's gene check and found that the mutated gene is the TS2 gene. However, not all TS2 genes were mutated. This suggests to the experts that the mutation occurred after Melissa's conception. This would mean Melissa's parents do not have TSC. It also means that the chances of Miles having TSC are reduced to less than 1 in 2.

Anyway, we have decided not to get Miles' genes tested as this could have implications in the future with certain insurances. We were told that some insurance companies might refuse to offer insurances in the future, including life insurance, if the applicant has had DNA testing, and that is what the gene test is. We are happy carrying on not even thinking about it. Miles makes it very easy for us to forget about all that.

x

MONDAY, 18 AUGUST 2008

Last Tuesday Melissa was admitted into Addenbrookes. Her breathing became a lot worse the last couple of weeks, and we decided to let our transplant coordinator, George, know. It was really to give a little reminder that we are really struggling along—sometimes we wonder if it's a bit of out of sight, out of mind. Anyway, his reaction was to immediately contact Addenbrookes and get Melissa checked out.

Melissa needed an x-ray to determine whether there was any sign of a pneumothorax or build up of chyle in the chest cavity that could explain the deterioration. If there were no such signs, it sounded like the Freeman Hospital wanted to transfer Melissa straight up there where she would have temporary treatment whilst waiting for the transplant!

The x-ray showed nothing. They wanted to make sure with a CT scan the following day. The CT scan also showed nothing (well, there was a minimal build up of chyle, but this came and went all the time). This meant that the whole problem is the LAM progressing to its end-stage.

We were expecting then to head straight up to Newcastle BUT plans changed when Newcastle received the results of Melissa's blood gasses. Her carbon dioxide levels were not quite as high (bad) as they had anticipated, and so they were happy for Melissa to go home if she was comfortable with that. They have assured us that Melissa is high up on the agenda for transplant now.

Coming home was a bit of a disappointment. Melissa was not particularly comfortable with that at all. She hasn't been comfortable for the last year. There were pros and cons with a direct transfer to Newcastle, but we thought the pros were better! The good thing about coming home is that we spend more valuable time with Miles—and that is obviously a very good thing! He is the best medicine of all.

The unfortunate thing about coming home is that sitting and waiting at Newcastle for a transplant to happen avoids the horrible scenario that so many transplant hopefuls must go through—getting a call in the middle of the night for a potential transplant, trying to sort out getting Miles to a safe pair of hands, bundling into an ambulance, and heading up to Newcastle at break-neck speed with all the stresses, worry, and preparation of what was about to come. There is the potential then that you will be told to turn around and go back home three hours into the journey should the donated lungs not be up to scratch or not make the transit. We know of other LAM patients, who have now had a transplant, going through this procedure up to ten times before the operation actually went ahead. This is an immense amount of trauma for a critically ill patient to endure.

We would also assume that by being up in Newcastle at the Freeman, taking up a hospital bed would mean getting the very next lung(s) available.

Therefore, Melissa is back home and of course finding things a lot harder than when she was at the hospital doing nothing! She feels like the rest of her body, especially her heart, is working overtime constantly in order to get the oxygen around the body.

It does sound like the transplant is imminent. It's all about keeping fingers crossed!

Miles is still doing very well—he's just had another tooth at the bottom and three at the top come through, and he didn't make too much fuss over them, just the odd hour here and there of crying.

We were in our local rag the other day—all good for raising awareness of organ donation.

Here's the link to register yourself as an organ donor: www.uktransplant.org.uk.

x

MONDAY, 13 OCTOBER 2008

Hi, everyone.

Yes, I know, I've been slack on the update, sorry. Unfortunately, it has not gone quiet because of green lights or anything, just really because there is not a great deal to report.

Melissa's condition, it must be said, has generally got worse, and she is able to do less and less. She is now pretty scared of the whole saga involved in trying to get out. She worries about being stuck in a public toilet, unable to pull the door open, and unable to shout for help.

Men can just whip it out and urinate anywhere—we are so glad we have a baby boy.

To be honest, Melissa is pretty scared of going to the toilet at home, let alone out and about.

There was a time back in August when we were on the verge of heading up to the Freeman to wait in the hospital for the next donated lung(s) to arrive. Whatever happened there?

Talking of Miles, the static body of insulation, he is doing very well. He is showing signs of moving at least a couple of inches at a time—we'll take that for now. He is still a very happy chap.

I was feeling extremely sick yesterday due to Melissa's sister getting me drunk (I didn't know what she was up to at the time as I'm sure you can imagine). I was so annoyed that I couldn't enjoy my day with Miles. Is this a sign of Old Git?

Anyway, more waffle to come but for now, bye.

x

SATURDAY, 25 OCTOBER 2008

Melissa's breathing took even more of a nosedive recently, and she was experiencing some sharp pains too. She phoned Angela at Addenbrookes on Thursday who wanted an x-ray that day and, hearing that Melissa's sats were in the mid-70s, organised a hospital bed for her too.

The x-ray showed a partial pneumothorax (lung collapse). Another chest drain was put in late that night. This is a job for the radiologists now. The only way they can make sure they are getting the accuracy they now need for Melissa's fragile lungs is by guiding the needle and tube in with the help from an ongoing CT scan. The procedure went well, although Melissa found it very hard to lie back so that they could slide her into the CT scanner.

I called the transplant team at Newcastle to let them know the latest, and they were happy with the chest drain option. They also mentioned, "Melissa's name is in red, right up there on the list." Angela seems to think that having your name in red means you're next in line once a match comes along. This is very nice to know, but hasn't Melissa been "right up there" for a long while now?

Melissa didn't sleep too badly considering there is a tube sticking out of her side, attached to a chamber! She started to breathe better, which suggested that the lung was re-expanding. Sure enough, the x-rays showed that the chest drain had done its job, and the lung had inflated. There was a little debate as to whether they were going to remove the drain Friday afternoon or leave it until Monday. Monday was agreed as the best option as that avoided weekend staff dealing with any complications should they arise from the removal of the drain. We were comfortable with that. Melissa feels more secure at the hospital anyway, and the oxygen she gets from the wall there is better than what she gets out of the machines in our lounge.

Saturday night Melissa had a temperature and was going hot and cold. She has been battling with a sore throat for a long while, and her throat now was very closed up. They took blood tests, and the diagnosis was unsurprisingly an infection. Perhaps we should be grateful the infection is not on the lung, especially as the wound from the chest drain was not dressed until sixteen hours after the procedure.

Melissa woke up this morning and could hardly swallow. She didn't want visitors and was just sleeping and reading today. I spoke to her on the phone, and she was on antibiotics for the infection. Her breathing did not appear to be affected by the infection. She sounded groggy though, to say the least.

Miles wondered where Mummy was this morning.

x

MONDAY, 27 OCTOBER 2008

Yesterday saw the end of the throat infection, marvelous.

Miles and I went up to see poor old grumpy bollocks. Life on the F6 ward is enough to make anyone grumpy, if I'm honest. Miles got a bit bored mid-afternoon, so we headed home. Melissa was doing okay, but that was yesterday.

Today Melissa could hardly breathe. It wasn't too bad while she was stationary but as soon as she lifted a finger or shifted her bum, she was working overload to catch air. It was distressing to the point of bringing tears to her mum's eyes. I ended up going back up to Addenbrookes late evening for a second shift of the day, leaving Miles with his nan and granddad. It turns out that Melissa has had another pneumothorax. Back down for another chest drain. At least I was allowed in this time rather than waiting for ages outside wondering how it was all going. It's quite an incredible procedure.

She immediately started to breathe easier and colour was re-appearing in her cheeks. There were even smiles.

We make this one chest drain number 8, brilliant.

Miles went to nursery today. He has started going in on Monday and Friday mornings with help from the Tax Credits benefit. After nursery, Nanny took him straight up to see Mummy. He went home with Nanny so that Daddy could go and see Mummy and not worry about Miles' bedtime. He is an adaptable little chap. Marvelous and brilliant.

x

FRIDAY, 31 OCTOBER 2008

Well the chest drain seems to be doing some sort of reasonable job. The lung overall is inflating although not quite fully inflated yet. It seemed to go up and down to a certain extent, which confused us all. Well, it confused me anyway.

Angela told Melissa yesterday that there is a separate additional pneumothorax—a very small one high up in the lung. Because it is small, they are reluctant to attempt to get a drain in. There would be too much of a chance that the procedure would be unsuccessful. It seems Melissa will have to grin and bear that one!

Melissa slept better last night (I don't suppose it was going to be much worse than finally getting some sleep at 05:00 the night before, she just couldn't lie back with the pains) and is breathing a bit better. She still seemed out of breath just talking to me last night though.

Miles and I are off to our friends' dad's funeral today. His mum's funeral was only six weeks ago. We're all looking forward to seeing the back of this year. We'll go and see Melissa after the service.

Come on Freeman, hurry up.

SATURDAY, 1 NOVEMBER 2008

Miles had his 1st birthday today!! What a star he's been. He's kept us going at times. He had a great day—we went up to the hospital, and Melissa was breathing well enough to take a big oxygen cylinder downstairs and sit in the cafe area where we had a gathering of Melissa's parents, her Nan, brother, and sister, and our friends Teresa and Iris.

Miles received really good and varied presents, and he was impressed with all of them. I think I probably enjoyed it even more than him—I banged on a drum for a bit and read some really cool books. Shame I couldn't quite fit into his jumpers.

He had loads of cards too. Once he'd finished opening and testing out his new gifts, he needed a sleep, and who can blame him. It was a lovely day and certainly was not spoilt by the fact we were in a hospital.

Miles will not remember it, but we certainly will. We have photographic evidence of it for him. Bad luck, Miles.

x

TUESDAY, 4 NOVEMBER 2008

Melissa had the chest drain removed yesterday. The lung has inflated completely. Her breathing, however, has not hugely improved. She remains on 10 litres/minute oxygen flow, which we are not able to generate at home as it stands.

The plan is to see how things go for a few days and see if Melissa is up to coming home. Reassuringly, they are not in a rush to send Melissa home.

Still no news from Newcastle.

An old school friend of Melissa's, Natalie, had recently caught up with Melissa and has since been organising a quiz night in Waltham Abbey on Friday, 5 December, in order to raise money for LAM and awareness of organ donation. Your £10 ticket includes entrance and a buffet style dinner. There is a raffle too and the prizes are absolutely incredible—we are amazed at the work that Natalie, her friend Rebecca, and her mum, Jill, have put into this and the strings they have managed to pull.

x

WEDNESDAY, 12 NOVEMBER 2008

Melissa came home last Thursday. Her condition was stable.

She is on 10 litres/minute oxygen flow now, and we have had the oxygen concentrators exchanged for the more modern powerful ones that can deal with this demand.

Getting out and about has become harder now. Melissa has adhered to the strict instruction for her not to do anything strenuous as this could provoke another pneumothorax.

Miles had an immunisation booster injection yesterday. He didn't bat an eyelid.

We've still not heard from Newcastle.

The quiz night has sold out (in days!) and Natalie, Rebecca, and Jill have done an incredible job in organising the whole thing—we met up with them tonight, and it's going to be a night and a half.

x

FRIDAY, 21 NOVEMBER 2008

Melissa has been short of breath for a while now. She really struggled on Saturday, and we were on the brink of going in to A+E, but she woke up Sunday feeling okay. She has had a very restful few days since then up until today, and this seems to have kept her stable and fairly comfortable (all things considered).

Today, however, she went out to see what the Isabel Hospice could offer her and although she liked what she saw (a bit of Reiki, Indian head massage, reflexology, art stuff), it seems that pushing a huge heavy cylinder full of oxygen around in front of her while being pushed in a wheelchair was not one of the best ideas.

This afternoon she was in pain and very breathless. She was starting to lose her voice, and her chest was stiff. We decided that I'd take her in to A+E and get her checked out.

I phoned the Freeman to keep them informed, and they mentioned that, assuming there is another pneumothorax, a discussion about pleurodesis would be a good idea. Pleurodesis is where the lung, once inflated, is deliberately stuck to the chest wall so that there is no chest cavity. This would eliminate the chance of another pneumothorax. This has not been done yet because it does make the transplant a slightly more tricky operation.

Then Melissa got worse. She couldn't really move from the bed, she suddenly went very hot, her saturation levels dropped to 85 percent; she lost her voice and struggled to get two words out at a time. She also had intense pains in her back, and she did not want me to leave the room (there's a first for everything).

We decided to call an ambulance at about 17:30. They arrived quickly and got Melissa on board safely. They even let us persuade them to take us to Addenbrookes (their instructions were to take Melissa to the nearest A+E and that would have been Lister, Stevenage; that thought brought shivers to our spines, check out the blog entry 13 October 2007).

During the journey, the ambulance crew increased Melissa's oxygen flow, and this seemed to help Melissa feel a little better. This immediately indicated to us that it was a pneumothorax. We got to Addenbrookes in no time. A blue-light journey comes highly recommended—intense driving!

Addenbrookes confirmed the pneumothorax. About half her lung had deflated. Another chest drain was inserted at 23:00.

The lung immediately started to inflate, and Melissa's breathing got a little easier. Unfortunately, the drain was inserted in her back rather than into her side. This meant it was going to be impossible to lie on her back for sleep.

Melissa's dad picked me up at 01:00, and on our way home, Melissa texted me to say she was being transferred from A+E to good old F6 Ward.

That's chest drain number 9. Almost double figures. She's so strong to deal with this time and again. I'm amazed.

x

Monday, 24 November 2008

Weekends are rubbish in a hospital. Nurses don't want to be there, and doctors don't know what they're talking about. The best advice I would offer a patient is to ignore them, or nod and pretend you don't want to knock them out.

At least there was a professor popping up on a couple of occasions. Prof. Redlock first reported to Melissa that the transplant team was keen to go for surgical pleurodesis. We were not too keen on this at all. Another operation, taking Melissa off the transplant list until recovered, and making Melissa even more weak than she already is. But they're the experts . . .

The next day, Prof. Redlock said that the team at the Freeman had changed their minds! Well, they are the experts. They would either go for a talc pleurodesis or just let things be. I'll try and explain. As I mentioned before, pleurodesis is where they stick the lung up against the chest wall to eliminate the chest cavity space. This should prevent pneumothoraces. They initially thought a surgical procedure was best because using talc is not particularly reliable. On second thought, they decided that using talc is, in fact, pretty reliable in cases like Melissa's where the lungs re-inflate well once the chest drains have been put in, and there are no signs of leaks. Using talc would not involve surgery. They would simply inject talc into the chest drain (already inserted into Melissa's chest cavity). This talc would irritate the lung, cause a lot of pain, and some inflammation. The drain would then be removed, and the inflamed lung should expand and stick to the chest wall.

Angela explained it's not an easy decision to make, and no one could really know the best way to go without hindsight. If Melissa decided to let things be, the chance of another pneumothorax was put at over 70 percent. This did not sound appealing.

However, with the talc pleurodesis, there is a chance that the inflamed lung would make breathing very difficult for Melissa (most people would be able to breathe okay but with Melissa's lungs in the state they are in, breathing could prove too difficult). In this instance, there would be a need for an external device to help Melissa with her breathing. A ventilator was mentioned previously, but Angela advised today that a ventilator would probably be a little too forceful for Melissa's delicate lungs. The machine could force oxygen down too quickly and rupture the cysts that are all over the lungs causing . . . pneumothoraces!

The team at the Freeman has mentioned to Angela a different device that will aid Melissa's breathing should this unfortunate side effect occur. Angela has not heard of it, and she was not

familiar enough with it to explain in detail. She mentioned the word Novolung (at least I think that's what she said). I have tried looking it up on the internet but couldn't find anything appropriate, so I am none the wiser on it. Suffice to say it will help Melissa breathing should she be struggling, although it does not sound an appealing prospect by any stretch of the imagination.

Melissa-the-Brave decided to go for the talc pleurodesis. If she decided to just take the drain out and let things be and then she has yet another pneumothorax, they will be performing the talc pleurodesis anyway.

It will be the law of sod that Melissa gets a call up for transplant this week, and we needn't have bothered with the nasty talc pleuro-thingy.

Miles and Karma seem to be getting along very well.

x

TUESDAY, 25 NOVEMBER 2008

Prof. Bridges at the Freeman has been on the phone to Angela. He shares Angela's concern that the inflammation caused by the talc could affect Melissa's delicate lungs too much for them to cope with.

He wants the pleurodesis to go ahead but instead of using talc, he has suggested using some of Melissa's blood! Apparently, this will stick the lung to the chest wall without inflammation of the lung.

I would like to know why we are getting so many mixed messages from Newcastle. It really is not helping us get our heads around things—we are constantly preparing ourselves for the latest way forward only to later be told of a change of plan. Surely one meeting with the prof, and the surgeon up at Newcastle would have come up with this latest idea before we were told of ventilators, surgical pleurodesis, talc pleurodesis . . . all of which are now abandoned ideas.

Anyway, enough whingeing! It's good news!

All going ahead tomorrow, as long as the sputum sent for testing comes back with no signs of infection. Poor Melissa is in for a very uncomfortable morning. Hopefully, her reward for bearing that will be a distinct lack of pneumothoraces in the future.

Miles likes his little drum. Daddy thinks he should get a full size drum kit for Christmas and leave it set up in his room.

x

Monday, 1 December 2008

Melissa came home Friday. The pleurodesis went well, and she didn't get too much pain (compared to what she's used to) so we were all pleased. Her saturation levels are at 88-90 percent.

However, as soon as we got home, Melissa was really struggling again. She worked out that it was panic. Friday night was horrible. Melissa couldn't get to the toilet in less than ten minutes from the bedroom (she now lives in the bedroom). The laxatives that she was prescribed to help her go when she hadn't been able to for almost a week had started working, and Melissa was really stressing about whether or not she could make it to the toilet all the time. I tried to tell her it doesn't matter if I have to change the bed, but dignity is a very strong feeling. This, along with the feeling that this transplant is not going to come in time, exacerbated the panic.

Saturday was a bit better for Melissa, thankfully. I had work in the afternoon but Spen, Tanya, and little Ashton (Miles' new cousin) came over to be with Melissa and to tend to Miles. Lucy relieved them of the nurse duties after a while. When I got back, Melissa was more relaxed, although still we wondered what she was doing at home!

Sunday morning a healer, Lydie, came round to see Melissa. It's all beyond me but Melissa felt a lot better once she had done her thing. Melissa was breathing through Lydie's lungs at one point! At this stage I'm very happy to go along with anything that has a good effect on Melissa's health. Meditation techniques were also discussed.

Then Melissa got a bit cocky and had a bath that totally knocked the stuffing out of her—she just has no strength at the moment in her legs, so getting in and out of the bath was a major struggle. The rest of the evening was spent recovering.

Today Melissa has taken her time with eating and going to the loo (the two things she is now restricted to apart from sleeping). She feels reasonable. When she is relaxed, she feels so much better. At one point, in a relaxed state, she guessed her saturation levels were up to 94 percent but in fact, they were still at 89 percent. Goes to show how the feeling of panic really can affect the ability to breathe.

Miles has not had good sleep at all over the last three days. His cough keeps waking him up and upsetting him. It also makes him choke on his food, and sometimes he'll bring it all up. Sometimes his bottle comes up too.

I'm knackered. Good night.

x

THURSDAY, 4 DECEMBER 2008

Karma, our amazing dog, was sensitive beyond belief and emotional too.

There was one time when she ran circles around Melissa out on a walk and pulled Melissa back to the house. Melissa went upstairs and had a seizure. Karma always knew something was up before we did. She always could tell friend or foe. She loved all three of us, and we loved her.

You can probably tell from use of the past tense that today Karma passed away. She died doing what she loved—chasing rabbits around farmers' fields. She slowed up and laid down on the edge of the field. I could tell something was wrong by the way she lay. I realised it was serious and carried her to the edge of the field onto the pavement. I called Mum to come and collect us, so we could go to the vets (she was not far away, looking after Melissa while I took Karma out). Before she got to me, Karma, in my arms, gave one last sad and almost apologetic yelp and that was it. I felt sick. It was, at least, a fairly quick ending, one minute chasing a rabbit, the next grinding to a halt.

She would have been nine in January. For a crossbreed, this is a short innings. We expected longer and looked forward to Miles growing up with her. It is such a shock.

The vets first suspected a heart attack but quickly felt fluid on the abdomen and agreed it was likely she had a tumour on her abdomen that must have burst.

We left Karma with the vets and went home to tell her mum, Melissa.

Not the news required for positive thinking at this already extremely difficult stage in her life.

We'll never forget Karma; she'll be missed.

xxxxxxxxxxxxxxxxxxxxxxxxxxxxxxxxxxx

FRIDAY, 5 DECEMBER 2008

Miles-stone! He moves. Yep, at last the boy wonder goes forward on hands and knees. It was pretty sudden, one minute rocking to and fro, the next he's off.

Now I'm sure most babies who find a new trick then go on to use it in abundance, in various ways—quick, slow, sideways etc. A bit of experimenting but not Miles. Nope, he crawled once, then sat down and thought, *That'll do*.

He's been poorly recently, and the doctor prescribed antibiotics for a chest infection a couple of days ago. He has thrown up quite a few bottles and dinners since last Friday. He seemed a lot happier yesterday and today though, so we hope he's over the worst. I wonder if the accidental diet has helped him to achieve crawling status.

Melissa has not been good at all. Panic, anxiety, and depression were all apparent before Karma died. Now they're out in force. This, in some ways, is scarier than a lung collapse. At least that can be fixed by shoving a tube in her side. This needs care that I, and F6 ward at Addenbrookes, cannot give her. The GP has prescribed a small dose of Lorazepam, small enough to not trouble her breathing further. We'll see if that has any effect. We are also going to take up the recent offer of a bed at the Isabel Hospice in Welwyn. There they have the medical awareness of a hospital (doctors and nurses) with therapeutic benefits too. As an inpatient, Melissa will be privy to a psychologist specialising in coping strategies for patients with terminal illnesses as well as Indian head massages, Reiki, reflexology, relaxation and visualisation sessions, gentle yoga, etc. If she doesn't like it, she can leave when she likes. There is a children's play area, so Miles won't get bored and need to head off after just a couple of hours. All sounds quite ideal at the moment.

x

SATURDAY, 6 DECEMBER 2008

Melissa was awake at three o'clock this morning and couldn't get back to sleep with her breathing a lot worse. Her saturation levels had dropped to 82 percent, and we called an ambulance at about 06:45. Straight up to A+E—the ambulance crew thought this might be an infection as Melissa has been coughing up dark-coloured phlegm. It was the usual routine—observations, blood gases, swabs, x-ray.

Then we had the news that the x-ray showed another pneumothorax, quite a big one, on the left side. This was the side that has only last week had the blood pleurodesis to prevent further pneumothoraces.

So, another CT scan-guided chest drain procedure. This was the most traumatic so far. Melissa froze in an upright sitting position, and it took a lot of calming and convincing to get her to lie flat so that she could be scanned. It was panic, pain, and anxiety along with a high heart rate, fear, and a lot of sweating.

The radiologist, Marcus, did a fantastic quick, efficient, and neat job, getting the chest drain in and quickly releasing air from Melissa's chest cavity. The improvement with her breathing would not be instant as it sometimes the lung takes time to inflate after it has been depressed for a length of time.

Back to her space in A+E while we waited for an available bed in F6 ward. I had to leave Melissa at this point to go to work, but at least I left her looking quite a bit more comfortable than she did on arrival. Melissa's mum and dad were on their way up not so long after too.

I spoke to Melissa this evening, and she sounded quite relaxed and tired. She had managed to lay on her back for a short snooze—quite an achievement with a tube sticking out of her back, and she was confident she would sleep well, having not really had any sleep for the last two or three days.

I believe the picture is showing you chest drain number 10. It looks a bit like Melissa has been riddled with machine gun bullets in her back and sides.

Melissa is desperate to get the call for transplant while she is in Addenbrookes. She does not want to go home. It's too scary, constantly trying to work out feelings and pains, diagnosing everything yourself, and then going through this turmoil every time something goes seriously wrong. Isabel Hospice sounds very appealing, but we need to find out if they can keep Melissa there for the duration and not just for a seven-day stay.

x

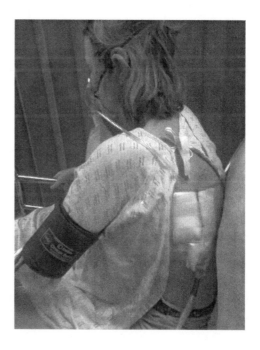

SUNDAY, 7 DECEMBER 2008

Melissa had a good sleep last night and seemed a lot more relaxed this morning. She was still struggling to breathe when she needed to transfer her bum from bed to commode and back again. She's had Sunday roast today—does that sound appealing? Well, you should see it. It's actually one of the better dinners she gets, but I'd rather eat what's in the commode.

Anyway, during the afternoon, Melissa had some sharp pains, and she was finding it much harder to breathe. She had an x-ray but this was inconclusive. She was sent down for a CT scan. Indeed, there was a problem. The latest drain had been put in close to the shoulder blade. Mistake. Melissa's shoulder blade soon created a kink in the tube internally, and this forced the lung to collapse slightly. As a temporary measure, they wriggled the tube about a bit and un-kinked it. Sure enough, the air escaped and lung re-inflated. They wanted to put a new drain in, through Melissa's side (why didn't they do that in the first place?) but couldn't because there was no air left to aim for—it all escaped when the existing tube un-kinked. There is a high chance Melissa will have yet another chest drain inserted when this one fails again due to shoulder blade intervention.

There is a very small chance the lung will stay up and heal if Melissa keeps her shoulder blade still for forty-eight hours. They must have been joking when they said that, right?

We should be getting some advice on what to do with Melissa's lungs (once the lungs have inflated and healed) tomorrow. As much as it didn't work this time, I think we would both prefer to try the pleurodesis with her own blood again. We have read about pleurodesis with talc and how the irritation from using it can occasionally cause a fatal reaction. Melissa's body is not strong enough for surgical pleurodesis. Anyway, we'll see.

   x

MONDAY, 8 DECEMBER 2008

The radiologist did not put a new drain in last night because the (inevitable) pneumothorax was actually a small one and they didn't feel confident trying to get a new drain in.

Now Melissa has to wait for a nice big pneumothorax that started to happen in the morning, more severe breathlessness and pain. It's like being tortured—knowing it's going to happen and then letting it happen in a long drawn out fashion.

By mid afternoon, Melissa was taken for the insertion of chest drain number 11. Melissa had been crying most of the day. Her friend Ros turned up just in time to dish out some love and calm and accompany Melissa down to radiology. That was a blessing. I was at home trying to get some rehearsing done—taking advantage of Miles going to nursery.

Another horrible ordeal but at the end of it, Melissa has a chest drain inserted in a sensible position, with air escaping and lung inflating.

Melissa's mum arrived to welcome Melissa back into her room. Not long after, Angela came along for some frank discussions. She had already told Melissa and me that we should prepare ourselves for every eventuality, including the potentially donated lungs not becoming available in time, but to say it again, with Melissa's mum there, was very hard to take for both of them. I'm sure a necessary conversation but not very pleasant.

I think Angela has become close to Melissa and is trying hard to do all the things that she feels Melissa needs, but we wonder if a palliative care team would be better for us, with these types of conversations in mind. Angela is, in fact, organising a meeting for us with the palliative care team on this subject. I think both Melissa and I do well thinking positively and not dwelling on the darker possibilities, but you never know, the meeting might help a little—anything is worth a try!

They plan to proceed with another blood pleurodesis tomorrow, assuming the lung stays inflated.

What a dreadful day.

x

TUESDAY, 9 DECEMBER 2008

Thank goodness, we've left yesterday in the past. Today Melissa was breathing okay and felt quite relaxed.

They left the pleurodesis until the evening. I think the logic was to wait until the blood thinning injection had left the body.

The pleurodesis seemed to go well until Angela came round half hour later. We were happily chatting about a few things, but then Melissa started to find it hard to breathe. Angela decided to open up the drain to see if it would offer relief (the drain gets left in but closed off at the valve after pleurodesis for about two hours, then re-opened to drain excess fluid from the procedure). It did help Melissa for a bit, and Angela noted that there were bubbles in the chamber, indicating a release of air out from the chest cavity. In theory, air should not have been there. Angela said something about some of the limited literature on this mentioning that blood pleurodesis could heal constant air leek. So, it was left.

Angela went home at about 19:00. In fact, every doctor in the hospital went home except one. Melissa's breathing became worse, and she and was struggling to breathe by the time a junior doctor got to her. She ordered an x-ray. She didn't know what to do, and the x-ray was unclear and inconclusive. She bleeped the one doctor in the whole hospital who said he would come up and see Melissa but had to deal with a few emergency calls at A+E first.

The chamber was bubbling away at times. We're pretty confused about this.

After hours and hours of tears and struggle, there was still no sign of the doctor. Melissa then had to deal with going to the toilet. Getting on to the commode was a harrowing experience. But, sitting on the commode, she suddenly could breathe easier. Taking things very easy, Melissa eased herself back onto the bed, and sure enough she felt like she could actually lay down. And possibly even . . . relax!!

I left at 03:00 and, although things didn't stay as good as that, they were an awful lot better than an hour before. There was still no sign of the doctor. I spoke to Melissa when I got home, and she was okay and thought that some sleep was a definite possibility. There was still no sign of the doctor.

If I didn't realise it before, I certainly realise it now—the NHS is stretched.

x

FRIDAY, 12 DECEMBER 2008

Another attempt at a blood pleurodesis is planned. Melissa's lung has gradually been inflating at a slow rate. The chamber was last seen bubbling at 03:00 Thursday morning. Therefore, they preferred not to do the pleurodesis today in order to give more time for the lung to establish itself as inflated.

They propose to do it tomorrow. A Saturday? No, thanks— you would have thought they would learn from the last one they tried that it is not a good idea to carry out a procedure like this without senior doctors around. We'll ask them to wait until Monday (assuming we actually get to speak to someone about it).

They inserted a pick line into Melissa for IV antibiotics today. This seems to be a measure to get rid of a persistent cough. However, it is very unclear as to whether Melissa has an infection or not. If not, why would antibiotics get rid of a cough? Is this just a preventative measure? If so, have they checked with the transplant team to see if they are happy to operate with a pick line in? If she has an infection, have they told those at Newcastle? Melissa would be suspended from the transplant list if so. Would someone like to explain this to us, please? It just feels like no one understands the greatness of the implications should Melissa be suspended from the transplant list.

All communication has vanished it would seem. Melissa has not seen Angela at all over the last couple of days. Not many doctors like to talk to us because I think they feel they are a bit out of their league with Melissa's condition. I asked the SHO (junior doctor) if she would come and talk to me about it all at about 12:00 today. Needless to say, I didn't see her again. This is not helping me persuade Melissa that they have not all given up on her like she thinks.

We spoke to Emma from Palliative Care today, and she hopes to help the communication issues. She told us that a registrar will be coming to see us later on.

We also had the ward manager and representatives from the Patient Advice and Liaison Services of the NHS (PALS) come in to iron out a few issues, such as the nurses on F6 Ward not realising that Melissa only has half an hour to get out of the ward and into an ambulance if she gets a call for transplant. It was only by chance that Melissa found out this was the case.

We only feel comfortable when Angela is in the same room as Melissa at the moment. Not many others seem to have a clue.

Oh well, life goes on . . . just.

x

SATURDAY, 13 DECEMBER 2008

We did manage to track down the SHO for some info late last night. All the registrars had gone home.

She said the bloods have been tested, but the markers are not up, and there is no sign of infection. Melissa does not have a temperature so again this suggests there is no infection. However, the dark sputum Melissa is coughing up does indicate infection. They are giving IV antibiotics to blitz this. The transplant team is apparently aware of everything that is going on and is happy. More importantly, Melissa has not been suspended from the transplant list, or so the SHO says. We have phoned the transplant team, yesterday and today, and left messages for them to contact us just so we hear that from the horse's mouth, but they have not returned the calls.

Due to Melissa's cough rumbling on, it was agreed that the pleurodesis should not happen just yet and will likely happen Monday. The cough could have agitated the procedure before. We were obviously pleased about that.

x

SATURDAY, 20 DECEMBER 2008

The pleurodesis has not happened yet. The cough Melissa has had has taken longer to clear up than we all hoped.

Also, over the last three or four days Melissa has not had much sleep at all as she has been kept awake with painful heartburn and indigestion. Today, her breathing felt much more difficult too, and she thought she might have had another pneumothorax. So another day, another x-ray and yep, another pneumothorax.

This seemed strange at first as Melissa has a chest drain in already, so in theory any air leek should have come straight out into the chamber. We were told that the lung had stuck in part when the last pleurodesis was attempted, which is good news in general, but it created two separate areas of chest cavity. One of those has just captured the air leek and depressed the lung. The other already has a chest drain in. The plan of action was to go down to radiology where they could look in detail using the CT scanner, possibly with a view to inserting another drain. They might be able to take out the existing one (surely a bad idea?).

I was at work while Melissa had the CT scan analysis.

Her mum and Miles were thankfully with her to go down to radiology—that place is feared by Melissa these days, just lying down to go through the scanner is a major challenge, then they get to work . . .

When I finished work, I phoned Melissa, and she was okay with her lung inflated again. They had decided against a new drain and just wriggled the existing one about until the trapped air came out. Melissa is unclear how this tied in with the above theories, and I haven't got a clue! We'll find out tomorrow.

Anyway, the indigestion has gone, and Melissa is breathing easier again. Hopefully, she'll get a nice long sleep in tonight.

We'll also wait to see if this has put a spanner in the works as far as the latest plan to do the pleurodesis on Monday.

x

SUNDAY, 21 DECEMBER 2008

Today was again eventful. At 06:00, I got a text from Melissa asking me to get in as soon as possible. Her lung had collapsed. I managed to get to Addenbrookes by 07:00, and the usual pains and difficulty in breathing were evident. The doctors were pretty quick to give Melissa attention, and the plan was to go down to get a CT scan and work out the best plan of action while down there. They wanted to wait for a second radiologist to arrive at the hospital for discussion, and he would be there within the hour.

During that hour, there was a lot of bubbling in the chamber, and Melissa's lung was inflating! By the time she was down at the scanner, there was just a little pneumothorax left. The decision was made to leave it. It was explained very clearly by one of the radiologists that Melissa's lungs were extremely fragile and that they were getting to the point where any further chest drain insertions or wiggling or any kind of general interfering with her lungs would come with a high risk of serious damage. Where the pneumothorax was so small, the risks get higher. The analogy is that Melissa's lungs are like tissue paper, with a chest drain tube being like a razor blade, such is the fragile state of her lungs. Lacerating the tissue paper would be disastrous.

Melissa also has a build up of air bubbles forming just under the skin around her neck. This is called surgical emphysema and often happens with chest drains that are inserted in the front. It has caused her throat to swell and ache, and it's hard for her to hold her head up.

At 12:30, Melissa's lung went down again. We were just wait-ing for it to happen really. After a while, at about 14:30, the drain started to bubble a little but not much. We experimented by trying to move about a bit. This was obviously very difficult for Melissa to do, but she managed it a bit. It seemed that when she lay back, most bubbles came out. This was unfortunately the most painful position for Melissa to be in, but the more the bubbles came out, the more the lung inflated.

By 15:00, the lung was probably up again (except for the little pneumothorax at the top of her lung that will be hard to get rid of). We saw a doctor who explained that when Melissa leant back the air that was trapped at the back was squashed around to the front, where the drain is, and therefore the air escaped through the tube. Simple really. Why didn't he let us know this before? He also mentioned that the quicker the air is removed from the chest cavity, the less likely the surgical emphysema would build up. Even more reason to let us know the quickest and best way to get the air out. Still, we know now so we're a little more prepared.

The only plan of action they are happy with now is full of hope! They really want the lung to inflate totally, including the tiny pneumothorax at the top of her lungs. They hope that the lung remains inflated for twenty-four hours while they shut of the drain valve. Then they can proceed with blood pleurodesis (third attempt) and hope that doesn't cause another pneumothorax. If we get to the lung totally inflating stage I'll be amazed, let alone the rest.

I've got myself a mattress, and I'm staying in the room with Melissa tonight. I've managed to convince Melissa that there is nothing better on the TV than *Match Of The Day* later on tonight, so I feel like I'm on holiday. All I seem to do at home is catch up with menial chores. I doubt very much if Melissa gives a crap about what is on TV at the moment.

Miles seems to have his nasty cough back and didn't hold down his lunch. He is with his nan and granddad today. I can't believe after two courses of antibiotics, it has returned.

x

MONDAY, 22 DECEMBER 2008

Night nurses don't seem to care if you want to sleep, they'll continue to slam cupboard doors, etc. Melissa is used to that, but her cough kept us both awake. All in all, not much sleep then.

The lung collapsed three times today. This is horrendous. A new plan was discussed. A bit sketchy and a lot more luck than judgment, the new plan was to wait for a time in the day where Melissa was feeling reasonable and the lung more up than down. Then they will go ahead with a blood pleurodesis, leaving the drain open, not closing it off for a couple of hours like usual—this may have caused the pneumothorax on the last attempt at pleurodesis.

We were told that Melissa would be no worse off but could end up better off. It might only stick part of the lung to the chest wall, but that would be considered progress of sorts.

The procedure went ahead at about 17:00. Out came 100 ml of blood from the arm. Then the blood was pumped into the chest drain. The drain was left open and at first, there was no bubbling, hardly any blood coming back out down the drain and all was looking good. During the next thirty minutes, the drain was flushed a couple of times to ensure the blood would not clot in the drain itself and block the drain, but there were a few bubble sightings.

At this stage, Melissa was in quite a bit of pain, and her breathing was still difficult. The pain was possibly something to expect after the procedure, but the difficulty in breathing was not expected. Time went on, the pain remained, and the breathing still difficult. Then more bubbles as air was escaping—as there was not supposed to be a gap for air in the chest cavity, we took this as not working 100 percent but still hoped some of the lung got stuck. Melissa's lung eventually inflated (whether fully or not is hard to say, but I doubt it).

I stayed with her over night again, and we both got a slightly better sleep than the previous night.

We feel like the transplant team at the Freeman Hospital does not remember us. This, I am sure, is more to do with us being terrified of the current state of events.

x

TUESDAY, 23 DECEMBER 2008

The lung went down again this morning. This happened just after she had an x-ray. The way everything is happening has to change—it's no good at all saying we'll x-ray you in the morning because at 09:00 the lung will look different than at 10:00 and different again at 11:00. Melissa is pissed off and is going to knock someone out soon. I'm beginning to hope it will be me.

What needs to happen is the second Melissa says her lung is deflated, a portable x-ray happens within five minutes. The results will need to be processed and looked at immediately. If the pneumothorax is big enough, Melissa will need to be down in Radiology having a CT scan guided chest drain inserted within ten minutes. There is, of course, no chance whatsoever of this happening.

At 11:30, Melissa's lung was still down. This had been a long and particularly painful one, possibly something to do with the pleurodesis. The doctor came round to say that she will be talking to Angela about possibly inserting a new wider chest drain into the same place as the existing one. They could use the existing one as a guide to get the new one in and voila, a new wider drain getting air out easier and quicker.

Then Melissa suddenly had a big lung collapse. Hands to the pumps, and 100 percent oxygen replaced 60 percent. Melissa was sobbing at this point. The doctors called for an x-ray immediately. This is not immediate though, and in the fifteen minutes it took for the x-ray machine to get to Melissa, the lung had inflated. The x-ray machine was told to go away! The bubbles came fast and furiously, the lung was up, and Melissa was feeling better than she had all day.

Angela came along and had a new plan. It sounded quite scary but a plan nonetheless.

She had booked Melissa in at radiology at 15:15. The radiologists were reluctant to do any further intruding into Melissa's chest cavity for fear of damaging the delicate lungs, but Angela herself was prepared to stick another, wider drain in. The scary part was the fact that she was going to induce a lung collapse by simply shutting off the drain and waiting.

Off we went at 15:15. Angela wouldn't let me in but by all accounts, she did a great job. Melissa was braver than ever, having her lung collapse intentionally, then lying on her back, a position that makes breathing even harder, while Angela did her handy work and inserted Melissa's twelfth chest drain. Then the old drain was removed, which was a struggle for the team! The local anaesthetic was not particularly effective either—this was because the surgical emphysema was spreading it all over her front. Amazing.

After all that, Melis came out smiling. Her lung was completely inflated for the first time since Saturday the thirteenth. She was in a lot of pain but could breathe a whole lot easier.

Back to F6 and she ate her dinner! This was some good news at last. Next stage . . . well, let's just enjoy this for a bit while the doctors have a think and see how things are tomorrow.

x

WEDNESDAY, 24 DECEMBER 2008

The worst day of my life.

Melissa woke at 04:30 struggling massively to breathe. It was obvious—Melissa had another pneumothorax. It was all way too much for Melissa who was now feeling this was turning into something barbaric.

Dr Baldock came to have a chat with us prior to doing something about the collapse. He told us straight and very clearly that we needed to make some difficult decisions. He asked us both to consider seriously what Melissa had been saying at times: "I can't keep doing this," "This is barbaric," etc. We needed to address the answer of how Melissa wanted to die.

I don't know about Melissa, but this scenario was not in my head at all. Maybe my positive nature is not such a good thing at times like these. Maybe I should have prepared myself a little more.

It boiled down to the fact that the team at Addenbrookes was satisfied that there would be no different outcome with each drain insertion. The lung would probably expand but then without doubt, the lung would collapse soon after as the lung appears to squash up against the drain when it inflates, blocking the drain and preventing the drain releasing the air from a collapsed lung scenario. The lung will collapse very frequently now as the cysts on Melissa's lungs are at the stage where they burst at will. LAM has progressed to this critical stage now.

Therefore, he told us that the options are:

1. To keep attempting treatment for collapsed lung causing

intense distress and pain every time Melis undergoes the procedure and every time the lung goes down again. The procedure itself is coming with a higher and higher risk of damaging the lungs further, and the radiologists have refused to continue attempting any procedures now. Continuing this way would give Melissa days, possibly weeks, to live in hope for a transplant, and they are very doubtful Melissa could even make the journey up to Newcastle anyway.

2. To let Melissa's body take its natural course and make her feel comfortable and relaxed with no stress or pain, having time to enjoy the company of Miles and me and her family. Leaving us the way she wanted to go, with no anxiety or screaming and with some time to be able to seriously discuss what she would like to happen when she goes, etc. This way also gives Melissa days, possibly weeks, to live but removed her from the option of transplantation, which may not be an option actually anyway.

Melissa chose the latter. I chose whatever she wanted and could not possibly put up any argument against her wishes having seen what she has had to go through over the last couple of weeks. Barbaric was close to the truth.

I knew we were at a point where the consultants were running out of ideas, but the shock of this conversation still managed to knock me sideways.

I cried a lot and am still crying a lot. However, in the meantime I'm looking at Melissa who now looks comfortable, with a little smile on her face, relaxed and relieved, and I know it's the best decision by far. I'm sad but a little happy to be seeing her like this. She is amazing even now. All the stuff she has been through took bravery beyond belief, and now she is being even braver. I think she has just accepted the cards she has been dealt. Even seeing her family and Miles this afternoon, she seemed accepting of this unbelievable situation. She says there is an element of not quite feeling it's real.

It dawned on me I hadn't seen her comfortable for a very long time.

x

THURSDAY, 25 DECEMBER 2008

Melissa woke in pain. This was not part of the deal. It was explained that they had to get the right balance of drugs that controlled the pain while not knocking Melissa out. Melissa was getting a constant supply of a cocktail of drugs that was to help her not feel pain and not become anxious. She was administered add-on injections when she felt pain and different ones when she felt anxious. It worked yesterday, but overnight the pain built up without her realising until she woke, suffering. The drugs then administered took a long while to kick in as they are designed to be a continuous flow.

She eventually returned to her comfortable state but was a lot groggier. The family turned up and we had about three hours of opening presents—and Miles! It was nice. Melissa had a rest halfway through, and we all went with the flow really. Couldn't have gone better all things considered.

Melissa received a nice amount of presents that were useful in hospital—books, pyjamas, a mug! The suitcases and theatre tickets were presents that were bought long before anyone knew of Melissa's current plight. This was awkwardly explained. The whole family did quite well at putting on a brave face.

Melissa is now trying to watch a soap opera, would you believe? However, I think her eyelids are getting too heavy, and I doubt she can make heads or tails of it.

It's got very hard writing this blog now, but perhaps it helps, getting down all the details, you lot all knowing . . .

x

FRIDAY, 26 DECEMBER 2008

Last night Melissa was up every two hours, sometimes more frequently, requiring add-on injections for pain and anxiety. I wondered if this was better than sleeping through it and having to catch up. The problem for me and especially Melissa was that although there was two hours of feeling peaceful, we were only awake when there was pain or difficulty in breathing, so it seemed to us that the uncomfortable part was constant. I only realised that myself once I got up this morning and had been by her side while she rested peacefully for a few hours.

The consultant came round and said that the syringe driver had been adapted again after last night's demands. His first guess of Melissa having weeks to days left had now altered to more likely just days left. Melissa's pain levels were very high, quicker than the doctors were expecting and hoping. The cocktail of drugs in the syringe driver was now pretty extreme in order to keep on top of the pain and try to avoid Melissa needing add-on pain relief injections. As a result of this, Melissa was a lot more drowsy and sleepy today.

Miles came up with his nan and granddad along with Spen, Tanya, and little Ashton. Melissa only managed a few words really. Mainly worrying about others, "Where you all going to sit?" Would you believe it?!

After the family left, Melissa wanted to speak to the consultant. A doctor came and Melissa asked if she could speed the process up. Melissa is hardly awake now and is frustrated that it's a struggle to talk. I think she does not want her family to see much more.

The doctor said that was illegal, but Melissa should not need to ask for pain relief frequently from now on.

   x

SATURDAY, 27 DECEMBER 2008

Sure enough, Melissa did not wake during the night to ask for pain relief injections, so the syringe driver must be pretty spot on with its dose now.

After a groggy morning, she had a lovely afternoon with Miles, her mum, her dad, and Lucy. She managed to drink a cup of tea through a straw, some words here and there, some smiles. Not much, but that'll do us.

How can I possibly expect my brother to enjoy his birthday today?

I hooked up a speaker to my laptop, so we've listened to some of our favourite albums today. Why didn't I think of that earlier? I'm not sure how much of it Melissa heard, but even if it was only bits and pieces, that's great.

x

SUNDAY, 28 DECEMBER 2008

I have been sleeping on a mattress next to Melissa's hospital bed for the last two weeks or so. This morning at 04:00, I was woken by Melissa's sharp intake of breath. I sat up on my mattress and leant on the side of her bed. Every now and then Melissa's breathing came to a standstill, but after twenty or sometimes even thirty seconds, her breathing started up again with a sharp breath. It appeared that her body was shutting down. I sat holding her hand and whispering my thoughts to her.

At 07:12, Melissa took her last breath. She passed away peacefully, holding my hand, just as she had wished.

She had endured an incredible battle against the symptoms of this terrible disease, ever since she was diagnosed with it during her twelve-week ultrasound pregnancy scan at the start of July 2007. During this period, she experienced the trauma of a burst AML on her kidney, chylothoraces, pneumothoraces, invasive thoracic surgery, pneumonia, C-diff bug, AML embolisation, blood pleurodesis . . . the list goes on. She'd had twelve chest drains inserted to either inflate her lungs or drain chylous fluid from her lungs.

During this time, she also managed to stay positive and jovial. She managed to be a fantastic mother to our baby, Miles. She even managed to join friends on the odd occasions—a wake, a leaving party, etc, where you'd see her in a pub with chest drain attached to her side, oxygen attached to her nose, and a glass or two of red wine attached to her hand! She was also an amazing wife to me. She was my best friend. Our most memorable and happiest day was our wedding day.

Her last few days could have gone one of two ways:

1) Continue the highly risky chest drain insertions to re-inflate a lung that was collapsing three times every day once the drain was rendered ineffective and probably not make it for much longer than a week with a glimmer of hope for a lung transplant that never came. She was at the top of the list for one since August. All this knowing there were huge doubts as to whether Melissa could actually make it through the journey to Newcastle's transplant centre.

2) Have a peaceful, restful last few days without feeling the struggle to breathe, enjoying relaxed time with her beautiful son Miles and the rest of her family, letting nature take its course with help to eliminate pain and anxiety.

Melissa was quick to choose the latter. For me, at first, it was difficult decision. She had been sobbing how she "cannot carry on doing this" and how "barbaric" the situation was and for some reason, I failed to realise she really meant it. The hope of a transplant kept me going, and it was hard for me to accept that the chances of that happening were almost non-existent.

Once I gave it thought, it became clear that Melissa deserved a break from the struggle at the end of her life. She deserved the nice things that came with a palliative care route. The minute I saw her in a relaxed state, it dawned on me how I hadn't seen her like that for way too long. The relief on her face was incredibly beautiful.

She gave me over ten years of love, happiness, and enjoyment, and of course she gave me Miles. So part of her will always live with me.

Thank you, Melissa, I love you and always will.

As a friend of hers said, "Rest in peace, Melissa, breathe easy."

xxxxxxxxxxxxxxxxxxxxxxxxxxxxxxxxxxxxxxxxxxxxxxxxxxxx

The Following Months

The day Melissa died was a bit of a blur. I watched as some nurses made her look nice, taking her oxygen mask off, cleaning up her face, taking her hospital gown off, and putting on some clothes they asked me to choose. I thought at first this was an odd procedure, but once they'd finished, I thought it was a nice thing to do.

I made a call to report her death to NDRI, an American company. They try to coordinate delivery of organs affected by LAM to research laboratories. One of Melissa's few wishes was to make use of her body organs when she had passed away, and she was keen that more research on LAM be possible at this tragic time.

I packed up all her things, and mine, and loaded up the car. I got a call from Angela offering her condolences. I drove back to be with the rest of Melissa's family at her mum and dad's house. It was such a sad and possibly even awkward atmosphere. No one knew what to say. Nothing could prepare us for that moment, and nothing could make things better. There was nothing to say.

Miles and I stayed there the night. In fact, we ended up staying there until the funeral.

Dad, Spen and I went up together to obtain the death certificate from Addenbrookes Hospital. It was a horrible drive back up there, a journey that was so familiar. While we were running through the details, it became clear that Melissa's organs were not removed for research. I was furious. This was the one thing that could have been done to make me feel a little better—knowing that Melissa had her wishes granted. It transpired that the organs had to be taken out of the body within eight hours, and as Melissa died on a Sunday, this was not possible. Weekends had long been feared by Melissa as the weekend staff rarely had enough knowledge to be able to deal with anything that came up. Now a Sunday had delivered its last blow. I really didn't care at that point that each copy of the death certificate I wanted would cost £4.00, special paper apparently.

The funeral was attended in force. Melissa had chosen cremation and had chosen the music. There was a huge turnout for the service and the wake. Plenty of red wine was slurped at the wake. Apart from a nappy change and a play with Miles here and there, I felt like I was mainly saying hello and goodbye to everyone.

I have kept a few sympathy cards. One from a LAM researcher in Finland came as a surprise. When we could, we sent her the containers full of the chyle that drained out of Melissa's chest cavity during her many chylous effusions. This chyle contained living LAM cells that could be cultured and grown. She mentioned how useful that was for research and that was really nice to hear.

I consider myself lucky with my work. I am mainly at home during the week, spending all that time with Miles. I then work over weekends when I drop Miles off to be with his nan and granddad. We have seen the back of the first year without Melissa now. Certain dates have cropped up that make things more difficult, such as her birthday (particularly poignant for her mum and dad), our wedding anniversary, Mother's Day etc. None of our birthdays have meant a great deal to us, and Christmas was obviously difficult too.

Miles, however, makes sure I have something amazing to live for. He has been a good boy from day one, and he continues to be fantastic. Melissa would be so proud of him and that is sadness and happiness at the same time.

From a selfish point of view, I feel lonely a lot of the time. I miss caring for and loving someone special, and I often wish I had Melissa to share decisions on raising Miles and, of course, to share the enjoyment he brings.

As for Melissa's parents, well, they have lost their daughter, and this is simply the wrong way round. They have also lost a bit of each other, and Dad has recently started receiving counselling. He is a very emotional character and has been pretty much knocked sideways. He recently had a heart attack. It was apparently a mild one. The CT scans did not show damage to the heart, and this indicates that in this case the cause of the heart attack was triggered by extreme levels of stress. This only happens in very rare circumstances. He is starting to work a day or two here and there each week now and seems to be recovering okay, although the drugs he must take now for the rest of his life are knocking him out a bit.

Mum has seen a couple of mediums—something she has always been sceptical of but Melissa was quite spiritual. Mum feels she ought to leave doors open for Melissa to make contact—for Melissa's sake. I am sceptical too, but I'm always very interested in the feedback!

Both Mum and Dad also get a lot of comfort and a lot of joy being with Miles.

Regrets and Corrected
Thoughts with Hindsight

I often think of two particular decisions that were made throughout the course of Melissa's final year that may have changed the ultimate outcome if made differently and, therefore, may have resulted in Melissa still being with us with a pair of transplanted lungs. I try not to beat myself up about them, but I can't help wondering.

The decision to be assessed for transplant at Newcastle's Freeman Hospital was a decision made purely by Melissa and me, albeit a well informed one. We were told she was at the top of the list, in red in August 2008. This meant she was apparently next in line for the next suitable set of lungs that came up. Assuming this was the case, I can't quite believe that there was not one donated lung that suited Melissa (who was a very average-sized woman with the most common blood group—and who was on the list for not only a double lung transplant but a single right and a single left lung transplant too) between then and December. I have heard of LAM patients waiting for transplant and being at the top of the list who have had up to ten phone calls in quick succession over a period of just a few months. A horrible scenario for the recipient—getting a call, only to be a false alarm due to the donated lungs being damaged in transit or for a number of other reasons. I wonder if the distance Melissa had to travel to get to the transplant centre put the team up there off of offering the lung(s) to Melissa. In this respect, I have often questioned our decision to choose the Newcastle transplant centre over the fairly local Papworth Hospital.

Another decision was, I suppose, more in the hands of the clinicians. I would never accuse the specialists at Addenbrookes of making decisions with their incredible expertise that were not what they firmly believed would be in the best interests of Melissa. There was a possibility they would perform a talc pleurodesis in August 2008. It was risky, and Melissa and I certainly didn't like the sound of it. They decided against it, as they did not think Melissa's lungs were strong enough to cope with the swelling, among other things, that the process would have caused. I wonder if the talc pleurodesis had gone ahead, would she have coped with the initial side effects? If so, she would not have had the constant lung collapses that eventually could not be re-inflated. This, I assume, would have given her a lot more time to wait for a transplant.

I realise now that some blog entries at the time of writing were full of high levels of emotion and were not logical. Reading back over the blog, I can say that with hindsight I stand corrected. This is particularly the case when I have mentioned it was not wise for Angela Davis, Melissa's lung specialist consultant, to talk to Melissa about preparing for the worst-case scenario of not getting a transplant in time. It obviously was the correct time to say something, it was just simply not what we wanted to admit at the time.

IMPACT OF ORGAN DONATION

Melissa would still be with us today if there were more organ donors in the UK. Being an organ donor is something that not a lot of us tend to think about. Not many of us come across the question of whether or not we would like to be an organ donor, and therefore, these decisions are not even considered. In this case alone, you can see that if Melissa had received a donated pair of lungs (or even a donated single lung) it would not be just Melissa's life that would have been affected.

I would have my wife back whom I loved so much, and I miss every day. She gave me her love, happiness, laughter, and she gave me Miles. She gave me a balance to my personality, and we were a great team. Stating the obvious, my life would be a load easier too! Organising a baby sitter for Miles every time I have a gig is not always that easy. Just little things like popping out to the shops are difficult. My day-to-day life would be dramatically improved.

As for Miles, well, he would have a mum. What price is that? I don't know if there is any proof of the effects of being brought up in a single-parent environment. I'm sure it's not as good as having both around. I suppose at this stage, he knows no differently, so any psychological effects that might happen have not happened yet.

Melissa's parents, it could be argued, have had the most upsetting trauma of losing their daughter. I am not sure if they have yet come to terms with it, and I'm not sure if that is something that they will ever be able to do.

It goes without saying that Melissa herself would benefit most. She would be enjoying the proud moments that Miles gives, enjoying her husband's company (sometimes), and the loving family she would have around her. She would appreciate the very simple things in life that most of us take for granted.

Melissa was only thirty-three when she died, and for young men and women, the chances of a successful operation and a greatly extended life term are very high. Other LAM patients have enjoyed a further twenty years and are still going strong since transplant.

A Tribute to Melissa

Melissa had quite an interesting mixture of attributes that I both admired and learned from.

Melissa Was Very Caring.

Her friendships required a certain element of intimacy. She liked a friend to talk openly with, about anything and everything. She loved the company of her friends' children too, long before she thought about having her own.

Arguably, her best friend was her dog, Karma. They looked after each other at all times, and Karma was suitably sensitive and emotional, sometimes warning Melissa of events before they happened.

Melissa loved her family dearly. She was extremely close to her mum, dad, brother, sister, and nan. It was new to me being with a family so much, and I grew to understand how precious that was.

She was a great mother too. Miles is a very lucky little boy to have had the instinctive, devoted, motherly attention and the unreserved love that Melissa gave him. Melissa was a natural, and Miles and I are lucky to have had Melissa around for such a delicate time in Miles' life.

Melissa was honest.

She was actually brutally honest, to the extent where you could easily be offended by some of her comments if you weren't familiar with her. I learned a lot from Melissa. With all my diplomatic ways in trying hard not to offend anyone, getting the point across was a struggle for me. In fact, at times, I didn't get the intended message across at all. With Melissa, the message came across loud and clear. Everyone knew what she was talking about, and everyone knew where he or she stood. There were no hidden agendas and no lies.

Melissa was courageous and brave.

Apart from the physical presence of an oxygen mask or a chest drain, you would never have known Melissa was ill. She was determined to carry on as if nothing had happened to her.

There was one time that she managed to wangle some hospital leave in order to attend a friend's wake, where she proceeded to polish off more than a couple of glasses of red wine. So there she was, in a wheel chair, with oxygen strapped to her back going up her nose, and a tube coming out of her chest into a chamber that sat in a bag strapped over her shoulder, with a large glass of red wine in her hand. The bag, by the way, was made by her mum out of dog footprint material!

That wasn't the only time she managed to get out and about—there was no stopping her. I did try!

Melissa had epilepsy, and she had brain surgery in 2005. The surgeon was removing two lesions on her brain—something he had not done before in one operation, but he felt it was the best chance they had of reducing and perhaps completely preventing further seizures. A couple of days after this major operation she wandered out of the hospital to a local store for a newspaper and a diet coke. People were crossing the road in an attempt to avoid this mad girl with bandages all over her head walking her drip on a trolley next to her. It was not long after the 9/11 terrorist attacks, so you can imagine what they were thinking.

I would not wish anyone to have to make a decision on how

they wish to spend their last few days at such a young age, but even this decision was made with unbelievable courage and calmness.

I know how effortless she made everything seem, how strong and determined she was to be with us and to continue her life though the paths she had chosen. She was determined to continue the new journey she had just set up and started with her beautiful creation, Miles.

Melissa was content.

She was content with the simple things life offered, not materialistic in the slightest. She would rather a cosy home than expensive clothes, cars, or restaurants. Even if it meant sending me into the bathroom to brush up on my tiling technique—where there was certainly room for improvement!

She didn't go out of her way to try and look beautiful, but she radiated beauty all the time. Maybe I'm biased or even well drilled?

Our wedding day was, without doubt, the best day of our lives. It was aptly held at Melissa's mum and dad's home with a marquee up in the garden. It was perfect. Very much helped by the sun!

The reason.

The real reason Melissa is no longer with us today is the fact that there aren't enough organ donors to cope with the demand. I hope to promote the discussion of being a donor and what that means. Anyone who knew Melissa and her family will already know exactly what it means. I'd like to let others know too.

Thank you, Melissa, for moulding my character into what it is today.

Thank you for joining me in leading our lives together as one.

Thank you for your caring, honest, courageous, brave, and content life that you offered us, which I embraced.

Thank you for battling against all odds for so long in order to try and share more time with us.

Thank you for Miles.

I love you, Melissa. I always will.

xxx

APPENDICES

Appendix A   Lymphangioleiomyomatosis (LAM),
              A Brief Background
Appendix B   Pneumothorax & Chylothorax Explained
Appendix C   Glossary

APPENDIX A

Lymphangioleiomyomatosis (LAM), A Brief Background

Lymphangioleiomyomatosis (LAM) is a rare disease that almost only affects younger women. It occurs in only one in 200 000 adult women, but it is a common feature in women with tuberous sclerosis. Tuberous sclerosis is an autosomal dominant genetic disease causing (mostly) benign tumours in many organs. Patients with LAM and tuberous sclerosis also have benign kidney tumours called angiomyolipomas. In LAM an abnormal clone of benign cells (called LAM cells) spreads throughout the body and grows diffusely in the lungs and lymphatic channels. In the lungs, LAM causes multiple lung cysts, probably through secretion of enzymes that damage lung tissue. The cysts reduce the capacity of the lungs to exchange oxygen and can also rupture, leading to pneumothorax (collapsed lung). Most patients come to medical attention with either breathlessness or pneumothorax. Occasionally, bleeding from angiomyolipomas or enlarged abdominal lymphatic masses is the presenting problem. The clinical spectrum of the disease is highly variable; some patients develop progressive respiratory failure punctuated by recurrent pneumothorax, whereas others stay stable for many years. On average, 10 years after the first symptom, over half of patients are breathless walking on the flat, a quarter will be using supplemental oxygen, and about one in 10 will have died. Diagnosis is made either by lung biopsy or from the combination of lung cysts visible on a CT scan and angiomyolipoma or tuberous sclerosis. Treatment has been mostly aimed at complications including pneumothorax and symptomatic treatment of breathlessness. Lung transplantation is an option for some patients with advanced disease. Impressive progress in the molecular pathology of lymphangioleiomyomatosis has demonstrated that LAM cells have abnormally high activation of the mTOR pathway (an important cellular switch which controls cell growth) resulting from defects in the tuberous sclerosis genes. This finding has led to trials of mTOR inhibitors in lymphangioleiomyomatosis that have caused regression of angiomyolipomas and possible improvement in lung function.

More information about LAM is available at www.LAMaction.org

Professor Simon Johnson

APPENDIX B

PNEUMOTHORAX & CHYLOTHORAX EXPLAINED

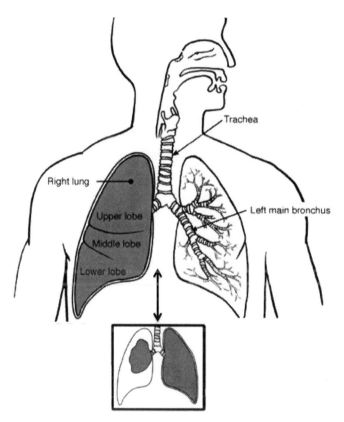

A pneumothorax occurs when air collects in the pleural cavity of the chest between the lung and the chest wall.

A chylothorax occurs when chylous fluid collects in the pleural cavity of the chest between the lung and the chest wall.

Both result in the lung being 'squashed' and therefore reducing in size/capacity.

Both can be treated with a chest drain, removing the air or chylous fluid and therefore letting the lung re-inflate.

APPENDIX C

GLOSSARY

Angiomyolipoma: Angiomyolipoma are benign tumours of the kidney and are composed of blood vessels, smooth muscle cells, and fat cells. Angiomyolipoma are strongly associated with the genetic disease tuberous sclerosis, in which most individuals will have several angiomyolipoma affecting both kidneys. They are also commonly found in women with the rare lung disease lymphangioleiomyomatosis. Angiomyolipoma are less commonly found in the liver and rarely in other organs. Whether associated with these diseases or sporadic, angiomyolipoma are caused by mutations in either the TSC1 or TSC2 genes, which govern cell growth and proliferation.

Although regarded as benign, angiomyolipoma may grow such that kidney function is impaired or the blood vessels may dilate and burst leading to haemorrhage. Large angiomyolipoma can be treated with embolisation. Drug therapy for angiomyolipoma is at the research stage.

AMLs: See *Angiomyolipoma*

C-diff: See *Clostridium difficile*

Clostridium difficile: Clostridium difficile is a species of Gram-positive bacteria of the genus Clostridium that causes diarrhea and other intestinal disease when competing bacteria are wiped out by antibiotics.

Clostridia are anaerobic, spore-forming rods (bacilli). C-diff is the most serious cause of antibiotic-associated diarrhea (AAD) and can lead to pseudomembranous colitis, a severe infection of the colon, often resulting from eradication of the normal gut flora by antibiotics. The C-diff bacteria, which naturally reside in the body, become overpopulated. The overpopulation is harmful because the bacterium releases toxins that can cause bloating and diarrhea with abdominal pain, which may become severe. Latent symptoms often mimic some flu-like symptoms.

Chyle: Chyle is a milky bodily fluid consisting of lymph and emulsified fats, or free fatty acids. It is formed in the small intestine during digestion of fatty foods, and taken up by lymph vessels specifically known as lacteals. The relative low pressure of the lacteals allows large fatty acid molecules to diffuse into them, whereas the higher pressure in veins allows only smaller products of digestion, like amino acids and sugars, to diffuse into the blood directly.

Chylothorax: A chylothorax (or chyle leak) is a type of pleural effusion. It results from lymphatic fluid (chyle) accumulating in the pleural cavity.

Embolisation: This procedure is a minimally invasive alternative to surgery. The purpose of embolization is to prevent blood flow to an area of the body, which effectively can shrink a tumour or block an aneurysm.

LAM: See *Lymphangioleiomyomatosis*

Lymphangioleiomyomatosis: Lymphangioleiomyomatosis (LAM) is a rare lung disease that results in a proliferation of disorderly smooth muscle growth (leiomyoma) throughout the bronchioles, alveolar septa, perivascular spaces, and lymphatics, resulting in the obstruction of small airways (leading to pulmonary cyst formation and pneumothorax) and lymphatics (leading to chylous pleural effusion). LAM occurs in a sporadic form, which only affects females, who are usually of childbearing age. LAM also occurs in patients who have tuberous sclerosis.

Pleural effusion: Pleural effusion is excess fluid that accumulates in the pleura, the fluid-filled space that surrounds the lungs. Excessive amounts of such fluid can impair breathing by limiting the expansion of the lungs during inspiration.

Pneumothorax: A pneumothorax refers to a collection of air/gas in the pleural space resulting in collapse of the lung on the affected side. The extent of the collapse of the lung is dependent upon the amount of air that is present.

Sats: See *Saturation Levels*

Saturation Levels: Oxygen saturation, commonly referred to as "sats," measures the percentage of hemoglobin binding sites in the bloodstream occupied by oxygen. At low partial pressures of oxygen, most hemoglobin is deoxygenated. At around 90 percent (the value varies according to the clinical context) oxygen saturation increases according to an oxygen-hemoglobin dissociation curve and approaches 100 percent at partial oxygen pressures of >10 kPa. A pulse oximeter relies on the light absorption characteristics of saturated hemoglobin to give an indication of oxygen saturation. An arterial oxygen saturation value below 90 percent causes hypoxemia (which can also be caused by anemia).

Thoracic Duct: The thoracic duct is an important part of the lymphatic system—it is the largest lymphatic vessel in the body. It is also known under various other names including the alimentary duct, chyliferous duct, the left lymphatic duct, and Van Hoorne's canal.

It collects most of the lymph in the body (except that from the right arm and the right side of the chest, neck and head, and lower left lobe of the lung, which is collected by the right lymphatic duct) and drains into the systemic (blood) circulation at the left brachiocephalic vein, right between where the left subclavian vein and left internal jugular connect.

Thoracic Surgery: Chest surgery

Tuberous Sclerosis: See *Tuberous Sclerosis Complex*

Tuberous Sclerosis Complex: Tuberous sclerosis is a rare, multi-system genetic disease that causes benign tumours to grow in the brain and on other vital organs such as the kidneys, heart, eyes, lungs, and skin. A combination of symptoms may include seizures, developmental delay, behavioral problems, skin abnormalities, lung and kidney disease. TSC is caused by mutations in either of two genes, TSC1 and TSC2, which encode for the proteins hamartin and tuberin respectively. These proteins act as tumour growth suppressors, agents that regulate cell proliferation and differentiation.

TSC: See *Tuberous Sclerosis Complex*

Lightning Source UK Ltd.
Milton Keynes UK
UKOW051525090112

185017UK00001B/30/P